"The single biggest problem in communication is the illusion that it has taken place."

George Bernard Shaw

How a Husband Speaks

*Leading and loving your wife
through godly communication*

By Ryan G. Frederick

LION PRESS

Published by Lion Press
a division of Vilicus LLC
2522 N. Proctor, PMB 461, Tacoma WA 98406
www.LionPress.org

How a Husband Speaks: Leading and loving your wife through godly communication, First Edition

Copyright © 2023 Ryan G. Frederick

Printed in the United States of America

All rights reserved. No portion of this book may be reproduced, stored in a retrieval system, or transmitted in any form or by any means—electronic, mechanical, photocopy,recording, scanning, or other—except for brief quotations in critical reviews or articles, without the prior written permission of the publisher.

Unless otherwise noted, Scripture quotations are taken from the ESV® Bible (The Holy Bible, English Standard Version®). Copyright © 2001 by Crossway, a publishing ministry of Good News Publishers. Used by permission. All rights reserved.

Scripture quotations marked NIV are taken from the Holy Bible, New International Version®, NIV®. Copyright © 1973, 1978, 1984, 2011 by Biblica, Inc.® Used by permission of Zondervan. All rights reserved worldwide. www.zondervan.com. The "NIV" and "New International Version" are trademarks registered in the United States Patent and Trademark Office by Biblica, Inc.®

Scripture quotations marked NLT are taken from the Holy Bible, New Living Translation. Copyright © 1996, 2004, 2015 by Tyndale House Foundation. Used by permission of Tyndale House Ministries, Carol Stream, Illinois 60188. All rights reserved.

Scripture quotations marked NASB are taken from the New American Standard Bible® (NASB). Copyright © 1960, 1962, 1963, 1968, 1971, 1972, 1973, 1975, 1977, 1995, 2020 by The Lockman Foundation. Used by permission. www.Lockman.org

Scripture quotations marked CSB have been taken from the Christian Standard Bible®, Copyright © 2017 by Holman Bible Publishers. Used by permission. Christian Standard Bible® and CSB® are federally registered trademarks of Holman Bible Publishers.

Author portrait by Deb Hurlburt. Used by permission.

ISBN 978-0-9974713-6-6

Library of Congress Cataloging-in-Publication Data is forthcoming.

24 25 26 27 28   7 6 5 4 3 2

For Nathan;
lifelong friend,
wise wielder of words

Let the words of my mouth
and the meditation of my heart
be acceptable in your sight,
O LORD, my rock and my redeemer.
Psalm 19:14

CONTENTS

Introduction...............................1

CHAPTER 1   The Word and the Flesh
Communication as a Marvelous Grace of God........9

CHAPTER 2   The Skill and the Heart
Your Words as a Unique Means of Loving Your Wife..15

CHAPTER 3   The Summit and the Descent
Learn to Know What You Don't Know............23

CHAPTER 4   The Interest and the Ant
How Tiny Gains Compound into Massive Results....31

CHAPTER 5   The Kilt and the Claymore
Disarming Defenses to Restore Marital Eden........39

CHAPTER 6   The Fog and the Friendly Fire
You Have an Enemy, and It's Not Your Wife........49

CHAPTER 7   The Goalposts and the Gaslight
The Scandalous Subtlety of Manipulation..........59

CHAPTER 8   The Tinder and the Storm
The Particulars of Communication Forestry........69

CHAPTER 9   The Wartime and the Peacetime
Responding to the Seasonal Sways of Married Life....77

CHAPTER 10	The Precision and the Power *Defining and Defeating the Husband Paradox*....... 85
CHAPTER 11	The Brothel and the Barn *Wielding Your Words to Build What is Good*........ 93
CHAPTER 12	The Lover and the Beloved *The Blessing of Communication Before, During, and After Sex*..................... 101
CHAPTER 13	The Clarity and the Pen *The Utility of Writing to Say All You Mean*........ 109
CHAPTER 14	The Road and the Ranger *How Tough Talks Bring About Unexpected Blessing*.. 117
CHAPTER 15	The Manner and the Method *Why (and How) Love and Truth Must Coexist*...... 127
CHAPTER 16	The Cliff and the Logjam *Breaking Free from Communication Deadlock*..... 135
CHAPTER 17	The Quest and the Query *Mastering the Art of Asking Good Questions*....... 143
CHAPTER 18	The Mold and the Map *Intellect Is Mighty but Wisdom Is King*........... 151
	Final Words *159*

INTRODUCTION

Good communication is the bulwark of every good marriage. And, as I'll make the case in these pages, sustained good communication is largely the responsibility of the husband—not *solely*, but largely. Thus, this book on the words of a wedded man.

So, if you're a husband who wants to improve his marriage by becoming a better communicator, you're squarely in the right place. I pray this book helps you to your worthy goal. Before you begin, a few things bear mentioning, starting with why this book exists.

REASONS FOR THIS BOOK

First, God cares how wedded men communicate with their wives. While many are quick to consult and cite scripture for ways to love well in marriage, not as many go to the Word for guidance through communication dysfunction. We know in our heads that God cares how we speak, but we don't often take the two or three steps further to understand just how that applies in marriage. God has clear and strong commands for how men speak to their wives, and this book exists to help us obey them.

Second, communication matters to couples. When we asked thousands of couples what they struggled with most in their marriages, the indisputable winner was communication. Not sex, not finances, not chores, and not even conflict. Communication. Why? Because every other area of dysfunction a couple faces always starts and persists through dysfunctional communication. If you can't talk, you can't walk. But, if you can talk, everything changes.

Which leads to my third reason for this book: By communication, marriages either flourish or die. If a couple can't communicate—by which I mean they can't share ideas, meaning, and experiences, not necessarily only through speech—they can't meaningfully work through anything. Not sin, not frustration, not life's big questions, not even dinner plans. Without effective communication, marriages die on the vine. With it, they have a chance. This isn't to understate the necessity of gospel centrality and Christ-like love—both are required—but only to say that communication quality is high on the list of determiners for marital success. It's a biblical notion borne out by data.[1]

THREE UNDERLYING PREMISES

Aside from assuming the truths of primary Christian doctrines like the Trinity, inerrancy and sufficiency of Scripture, marriage, and others, I've built this book on three premises.

Premise #1: Husband and wife are complements.

Stated briefly, I (as well as Selena) embrace the interpretation of Scripture—namely Genesis 1–3, Ephesians 5:22–33, and 1

---

[1]. Farah Haris and Aneesh Kumar, "Marital Satisfaction and Communication Skills Among Married Couples," *Indian Journal of Social Research* 59, no. 1 (January 2018): 41, https://www.researchgate.net/publication/324680369_Marital_Satisfaction_and_Communication_Skills_among_Married_Couples

Timothy 2:13—that affirms the husband as the head of the home and the wife as his helper. This topic is still hotly debated, but I won't do so here aside from one clarifying statement.

The biblical conception of head and helper is not one of power, position, or importance, but rather one concerning roles and responsibilities. This is the most common misconception, especially in our age of man bashing and patriarchy smashing. We must not let the evils of some men who have acted unbiblically stain our perceptions of genders and their roles. Biblically, men and women are both made in the *imago Dei* and carry equal value, worth, and importance.

In an essay titled "Male-Female Equality and Male Headship," Raymond Ortlund Jr. said it well:

> Responsible interpreters [of Genesis 1–3] do not advocate demeaning, oppressive "male dominance." They advocate selfless male headship, in which the man undertakes to serve his wife and family by providing the leadership that will glorify God and benefit them without regard for the price the man must pay to fulfill that responsibility. Headship calls us men to lay down our lives for our families.[2]

Within the complementarian understanding, I simply posit that one of the best and most opportune ways a husband can "serve his wife and family by providing leadership that will glorify God" is through the ways he communicates. This includes being

---

2. Raymond Ortlund Jr., *Male-Female Equality and Male Headship*," Bible.org, April 11, 2005, https://bible.org/seriespage/3-male-female-equality-and-male-headship-genesis-1-3.

the first to take responsibility for communication failures which may not be entirely his fault.

Premise #2: Communication is a grace of God.

The ability to communicate is so common we take it for granted. This, I think, is one of the reasons we don't excel as well as we could. Metaphysical and philosophical considerations aside, it is a remarkable thing that one soul can know another. And, the keys to such knowledge are the varying, wonderful faculties of communication. The first chapter expounds on this premise in greater detail.

Premise #3: Communication is a learnable skill.

I'm betting you heartily agree that communication is a skill since you're reading a book about how to do it better. The second chapter talks about this further, but for introduction purposes, know this: as you approach each chapter, do so without being a determinist. You *can* change, and you *can* grow into the kind of man who communicates well, regardless of your past, personality, or predisposition.

BOOK STRUCTURE

Knowing how the book is structured will help you get your bearings early and harvest the most from these pages.

Chapter Order

The order in which you read the chapters is flexible as long as you read chapters 1 and 2 first. As mentioned above, those chapters establish foundational premises that will help the subsequent chapters make more sense. Think of each chapter first as a standalone short essay, then as a part of a book. My aim is to give you arrows for your communication quiver that you can use as needed and at your discretion. The subtitles of each chapter should give you a good idea of the subject addressed. See one now that flips your flapjack? I say go for it.

Read in order or at random; just read chapters 1 and 2 first.

Application Questions

Every chapter includes questions to help you think more deeply and personally about the material covered. At times this may include a challenge (e.g., Write a letter to your wife). View the questions as tools to be used at your discretion, so long as they prove beneficial. What I mean to say is, don't let the questions or their rigor bog you down. Get through the book however you choose, but do get through it.

Devotional Supplement

There are eighteen chapters enclosed, which means it could be used as a three-week study (assuming one day off per week). Each day includes Scripture to varying degrees, so you will see clear lines drawn from the topic into the pages of God's Word, but it is no replacement for your own devotions.

If you do decide to use this book as a three-week study, plan on ten to fifteen minutes of daily reading and another ten minutes for questions in addition to your personal study and prayer times. I recommend slotting Saturdays or Sundays as your off days.

A FINAL ENCOURAGEMENT

Nobody needs help communicating when things are great. It's when things break down that couples realize they need assistance. And, many times, they don't fully realize exactly *what* they need. If communication is a problem, it's reasonable to not know how to put that exact problem into words. Which is precisely why you hold these words in your hand.

My entire goal for this book is to give you hope and tools for how you communicate and relate to your wife. Why? Because learning to communicate better with Selena changed our marriage for good. I want to share that not just so you can be happier but so you can live more united and on mission with Christ.

Our King is worthy and his work awaits. Sadly, I've seen too many men and women sidelined by marital misfires. A miscommunication unaddressed turns to frustration, frustration to bitterness, bitterness to isolation, and isolation to prolonged marital strife or an affair. It's tragic, but common. My hope is that by learning skills to prevail against dysfunction, distraction, and diversions, you will be able to get *at* your wife's heart. To know her, to love her, and to lead her in such a way that she *feels* known, loved, and led.

With all that, I'd be honored to pray for you.

> *Father, you alone are God, and you alone deserve glory. Thank you for the words you've revealed that we might know you and your will.*
>
> *Please, be with this man as he learns more about how to love his wife through communication. Open his eyes, sharpen his mind, and soften his heart. Make him attentive to your Word and diligent to apply all it instructs. I pray the coming weeks would be formative for him—so much so that his wife not only sees him change but feels it as well.*
>
> *All this I pray in the glorious name of Jesus Christ, amen.*

CHAPTER ONE

THE WORD AND THE FLESH
Communication as a Marvelous Grace of God

> In the beginning was the Word,
> and the Word was with God, and the Word was God.
> He was in the beginning with God.
> John 1:1–2

Communication is the process of one individual sharing information and ideas with another. Obvious, I know, but it's a profound thing. We take for granted the marvel it is to be able to communicate with the souls around us. Communication may be commonplace, but it's still miraculous.

Consider with me for a moment all that occurs when you communicate. As if without a thought, you abstract concepts from concrete things, encode those abstractions into words, and fire neurons in your brain that tell your tongue, lips, diaphragm, and vocal chords to constrict and flex just so in order to release energy in the form of sound. The sound reverberates through the surrounding air molecules until those sound waves enter your hearer's ears, causing their ear drums to flutter and pulse, which triggers their neurons to fire, thus detecting, decoding, and assigning meaning and then significance to your words in their mind. You've effectively shared a thought with another soul, all within fractions of moments and with little conscious effort. Not all miracles are rare.

Your ability to communicate with your wife is as marvelous as it is vital. Your words are the currency you exchange for access, knowledge, and connection to each other's souls. It's how you know and are known.

The entirety of this book is written to help you think about communication differently, intentionally, and with deep appreciation for all it is and *can be* in your marriage. The best place to start our journey is to understand the greatest miracles of communication in the history of creation: the transmission of God's inscripturated Word through the Holy Spirit and the condescension of God's incarnate Word, Christ.

OUR TRIUNE GOD AND HIS TWOFOLD WORD

How do we know God? Had he not revealed himself, we would not know him. And, of all the ways God could have chosen to reveal himself and his decree, he chose to communicate through the written words of Scripture and the incarnate Word, his Son. "Long ago, at many times and in many ways, God *spoke* to our fathers by the prophets, but in these last days he has *spoken* to us by his Son, whom he appointed the heir of all things, through whom also he created the world" (Hebrews 1:1–2, emphasis added). Additionally, and as a kind of precursor to both, we know of God (generally, not specifically) through the embedded God-glorifying groanings of creation itself.

Our Creator made everything in such a way that it all resonates unceasingly with his splendor. David wrote, "The heavens *declare* the glory of God, and the expanse *proclaims* the work of his hands. Day after day they *pour out speech*; night after night they *communicate* knowledge" (Psalm 19:1–2 CSB, emphasis added). His divine craftsmanship is so obviously visible in creation that, to summarize Job, "beasts and bushes teach of God's goodness and birds and fish declare it!" (Job 12:7–8). He is so abundantly evident that Job finally erupts, "Who among all these does *not* know that the hand of the LORD has done this?" (Job 12:9, emphasis added). Without uttering a word or sharing a thought, creation bellows without pause the magnificence of God, and this majestic music is readily heard by those with ears to hear it.

Yet, this God of ours, despite having revealed himself so thoroughly in his creation, still saw fit to communicate his character and decree through the written word. And when mankind failed to obey him—that is, to respond by joining creation in attributing to God the glory he deserves—we made ourselves objects of wrath. But he didn't leave us there. Instead of wrath, he sent his Son, the incarnate Word—the *logos*—to save.

In his noteworthy book *God's Word Alone*, Matthew Barrett writes,

> Scripture is the constitution of the covenant between God and his people. Therefore, to reject God's Word is to reject his covenant as well. Redemptive history demonstrates that the covenantal Word of the triune God proves

true. His covenantal promises, both spoken and written, will not fail, and nowhere is this more evident than in the incarnation of Christ, the Word made flesh.[3]

The mysteries of God's character and decree have been communicated to us (revealed) through the unmerited graces of God's law, the written Word, and the gospel of Christ, his incarnate Word. There is no greater or more staggering truth to behold.

JUST *AND* THE JUSTIFIER

What does this all have to do with communication in marriage? Aside from being foundational truths for the Christian faith, they're also foundational truths for how you communicate and how you *think* about communication.

Husband, consider this: not only did God give grace in order to be reconciled to us, but he gave *himself*. He spoke, then he satisfied his own decree. He initiated the relationship, crafted the covenant, then stepped in to satisfy its requirements. He did it with Abram as he passed between the splayed sacrifices in Genesis 15, and he did it finally in Christ, "to show his righteousness at the present time, so that he might be just *and* the justifier of the one who has faith in Jesus" (Romans 3:26, emphasis added).

Can you imagine a reality where God was a liar? Where his word couldn't be trusted? Imagine God promising and not fulfilling. Imagine God speaking unjustly or with haste. It's a terrifying thought experiment.

---

3. Matthew Barrett, *God's Word Alone: The Authority of Scripture* (Grand Rapids: Zondervan, 2016), 29.

A HUSBAND AND HIS WORDS

Just as God's words are intertwined with his covenant with his people, so are your words intertwined with your covenant with your wife. How you speak, what you say, your posture, how you listen, and when you respond… it *all* matters. Christ loved his bride even unto death, and you are called to do the same. This reality should permeate every aspect of your marriage, especially your communication.

In the perennial marriage passage from Ephesians, Paul charges husbands to love their wives and to give themselves up for her, just as Christ gave himself up for the church (Ephesians 5:25–33). Every believer, male and female, is called to die to their flesh and live for Christ, but the call to give oneself up for another as Christ did for the church is unique to marriage and isolated to husbands. Wives aren't told to die for their husbands as Christ died. Wives have their own charge. Dying is the husband's job.

Now, how does this inform how a husband communicates? It starts with recognizing that the communication buck stops with you. What I mean is, you take the primary responsibility for the habits and culture you form around how you and your wife speak to one another. Of course, she plays a massive role and I'll grant that she might be naturally better at it, but you're on the hook for making sure all goes well.

In the garden, God approached Adam. In your marriage, he will approach you. Will the words you say and the way you speak help you present your bride "without spot or wrinkle or any such thing, that she might be holy and without blemish," as Paul described (Ephesians 5:27)? You can't save your wife's soul, but you're called to steward it in such a way that it shows.

Your words can build up or tear down.

Your words can increase faith or leverage fear.

Your words can be filled with grace or dripping with gall.

God cares how you communicate to your bride. *What* you say and *how* you say it matters a great deal. She's God's daughter before she's your wife; steward her soul in a way that would make your heavenly Father-in-law smile.

SPEAK AS JESUS SPEAKS

Communication mastery is not only a matter of learning the skills, though that part is indispensable and comprises a large portion of this book. Mastering how you relate to your wife through words is rooted in understanding how your good God has related to you in Scripture and in Jesus. Start there. Look to Christ. Then, look soberly at yourself.

The rest of this book builds on this trite imperative: we must speak as Jesus speaks. Let your words to your bride be what God's words are to his, and may God's embodied Word, Christ, be your supertype—the perfect example and exemplar for how to love her well in communication. So, let me ask you,

Do you reflect Christ's likeness in how you communicate with your bride?

Does his voice resonate with yours?

Do your words echo God's true, loving, reliable, patient, and gracious decrees?

Whatever your answers to those questions, I'm betting that with this book, time, practice, and tons of grace, you'll be headed in the right direction.

> **KEY TAKEAWAY**
>
> Mastering how you relate to your wife through words is rooted in understanding how your good God has related to you in Scripture and in Jesus.

MEDIOCRITY VS MASTERY

Mediocrity	*Mastery*
Takes communication for granted; sees little opportunity in it	Harnesses the opportunity to communicate as a means to love
Relegates communication leadership to wife	Owns role as chief communicator; leads intentionally
Speaks only in ways that come quickly and naturally	Seeks to speak as Jesus speaks, carefully and with intention

APPLICATION QUESTIONS

Do you reflect Christ's likeness in how you communicate with your bride? Does his voice resonate with yours? Why or why not?

Describe what it could look like if you spoke to your wife as Jesus speaks throughout the pages of Scripture. Consider a few common communication scenarios where you're hoping to grow.

CHAPTER TWO

THE SKILL AND THE HEART
Your Words as a Unique Means of Loving Your Wife

> *Husbands, love your wives, as Christ loved the church and gave himself up for her, that he might sanctify her, having cleansed her by the washing of water with the word, so that he might present the church to himself in splendor, without spot or wrinkle or any such thing, that she might be holy and without blemish.*
> Ephesians 5:25–27

Two things are worth mentioning at this point.

First, communication is a skill that can be acquired regardless of your temperament. I say this to counter the notion that a man's personality determines whether he can effectively express his own thoughts and emotions or understand those of his wife. Though we may have stylistic differences based on personality, *every* man can learn to communicate well. Emotional intelligence and interpersonal acuity are not exclusive to any one personality type.

Second, the goal isn't to merely learn the skill, but to become the *type* of man who uses communication to love his wife well. Skilled communication does not a loving husband make! Master manipulators and sociopaths are adept communicators, yet they use their words as a weapon and an advantage for selfish gain. This must not be so in a Christian marriage. It *cannot* be so.

THE SKILL

My wife is tough as nails, but she shouldn't have to be tough on account of me. With me, she should be safe, at ease, and secure. She should be free to flourish as a well-watered vine, not one that withers, shrivels, and dies. This many years into our marriage, I'm happy to say that she's flourishing. I'm less happy to admit that it wasn't always the case, in large part due to the communication culture we had created in our home.

We've never been name callers or venom spewers in our marriage, but like all couples, we had our own special brand of communication dysfunction. Impatience, shortness, coldness, hastiness, laziness, and just run-of-the-mill unloving-ness are all weeds we've had to pluck and re-pluck from our shared conversation garden. In heated moments I was often so hasty to defeat her arguments with reason and logic that I forgot the woman behind them. Too many times my tender wife was caught in the communication crossfire, becoming a casualty of verbal war—where I sought to defeat ideas, but I left my best friend defeated in the process.

Thankfully, God has a way of growing us and showing us exactly how "love covers a multitude of sins" (1 Peter 4:8), especially *young* love. I'm not the man I once was. And, you don't have to be the man you are today for the rest of your life either. It just takes effort and unwillingness to settle for excuses, which is what we'll look at next.

ESCHEWING EVERY EXCUSE

It takes time to grow in the communication category and, tragically, many men never grow out of communication prepubescence. They can grow a beard, but their communication self is still learning to walk. It wasn't until my thirties that I finally learned how to articulate my emotions to Selena. I'm not proud of it, but it's true. Blame it on culture, upbringing, or what have you. Perhaps it's because on this topic, many men are fatalists. I know I was.

I am what I am.
I'm not a talker.
I'm wired this way.
I'm introverted.
I don't need to express myself.
She's verbal; I'm not.
I don't need to talk like she does.

Those are all things I've believed about myself at one point. But, in no other sphere of life would this type of futile, fatalistic reasoning fly. At work, if you lack skills to do your job well, it's expected that you will learn, adapt, and grow, or find another job. If a worker throws their hands up and refuses to learn, that worker's days are numbered.

Husbands need not be victims of their own inclinations. Every husband can grow into a better communicator. I'd even go one step further and say they *should*. It's part of the whole "husbands, give yourselves up" thing. No part of you or your marriage is untouchable by sanctification's sword. Which, for those being molded into the image of Christ, is incredible news.

THE COMMAND AND QUALITY OF A GODLY HUSBAND

As I mentioned before, the primary goal here is not to acquire a skill set; it's to become the *type* of husband who loves his wife well through how he communicates. This sort of objective fits well within Paul's directive to husbands in the book of Ephesians. It's a well-worn passage in every marriage book, but we must visit it often.

Paul, with a few strokes of his quill, raised the bar for all husbands to the standard set by the Son of God himself. No biggie. "Husbands, love your wives, *as Christ loved* the church and *gave himself up* for her" (Ephesians 5:25, emphasis added). It's a mountainous ultimatum with unparalleled implications, even for talking and listening to your wife. How might Paul's imperative apply to your marital communication?

First, behavior modification won't cut it. True change must well up from the heart by the Spirit after *first* drinking deep the water of Christ. Just as Jesus said, "If anyone thirsts, let him come to me and drink. Whoever believes in me, as the Scripture has said, 'Out of his heart will flow rivers of living water'" (John 7:37–38). Christ was speaking of the Holy Spirit which he promised to send (and did), and the heart transformation that would result. Being transformed by Christ is the first step in transplanting selfish desires with *selfless* ones. Which in this case, an otherwise closed-off, passive, and lazy communicator will now *want* to love his wife by *doing* the opposite. Changed hearts behave differently because they crave differently.

Second, with Christ as your fountainhead and the Spirit as your power, you must put your hands to the plow. Simply put, it's your turn to do the work necessary to actualize the change you now desire. Healthy communication skills don't build themselves no matter how Christian you are. Christ saved you free of charge, but he won't speak to your wife for you. That joy is yours alone to endeavor.

So, that's the secret sauce. To become the type of man who loves his wife like Christ in how he communicates, you must first go to him, drink, let the Spirit flow, and get to work. The work may not be easy, but the fruit is worth it.

THE PATH AHEAD

You and your wife are in this communication journey together, and certain challenges do abound. Depending on your situation, you may feel hopeless to succeed against them. You might feel like you'll never crack the ice in your communication cold snap. Or you may just be looking to bone up on your existing skills. Either way, the good news is that your marriage covenant is built for this. It's God's designated place for you to work out your faith alongside your wife in the safety and security of lifelong biblical love. Can you imagine doing it any other way? Take a deep breath; you're not alone. The Spirit is at work within you, Christ is contending for you, and your wife is standing beside you.

The two primary premises of this book are (1) communication is a grace of God (first chapter), and (2) communication is a skill that can be mastered (this chapter). Does this mean you'll never experience difficulty in the craft? Not remotely. But it does mean you can stop making the same mistakes and getting stuck in familiar ruts. Most of all, it means you have an incredible opportunity to love your bride more completely as Christ has loved you through the ways you interact. But once again, you *must* go to him first.

Fellow husband, are you going to Christ? Does he have your heart, your trust, your devotion, and your wholehearted obedience? Without Jesus, your most well-meaning fount will soon run dry. Your skilled behaviors will quickly revert back to familiar patterns and habits. But with Christ, the Spirit's deluge into every facet of your life can never be assuaged.

> **KEY TAKEAWAY**
> Communication is a skill that can be mastered regardless of your past, personality, or disposition, and growing in this area is perhaps your best and most immediate opportunity to improve your marriage.

MEDIOCRITY VS MASTERY

Mediocrity	Mastery
Comfortable with the communication status quo	Refuses to let past patterns determine future growth
Uninterested in growing into a better communicator	Recognizes the opportunity to grow into a better communicator
Blames communication difficulty on personality differences	Embraces the possibility for growth despite different dispositions

APPLICATION QUESTIONS

Reflect on how you have historically received, processed, and shared information throughout your life. What are two or three ways you can grow as a communicator in general?

List two or three ways you can grow as a communicator with your wife. Be specific.

CHAPTER THREE

THE SUMMIT AND THE DESCENT
Learn to Know What You Don't Know

Thus says the LORD: "Let not the wise man boast in his wisdom, let not the mighty man boast in his might, let not the rich man boast in his riches, but let him who boasts boast in this, that he understands and knows me, that I am the LORD who practices steadfast love, justice, and righteousness in the earth. For in these things I delight, declares the LORD."
Jeremiah 9:23–24

Seven days after having open heart surgery, I couldn't climb a flight of stairs.

Seven *years* after, I summited Mount Rainier. This isn't to say I'm awesome; I barely made it. Still, it was an emotional moment and a stark reminder of God's kindness and grace. It was also a reminder that mountain peaks are for visiting, not for living.

If you've ever flown over mountains (or climbed one), you probably noticed that their peaks are barren. Nothing lives up there. Not a tree, a bush, a marmot, or a goat. Sure, in the valleys and crags below, one might find signs of life, but on the peaks? Nothing. That's because peaks can't sustain life. They're too exposed, the air is too thin, and there aren't resources to forage or hunt. For avid mountaineers, there's even a point where the elevation begins to actively kill you because the air is too thin. This has been creatively dubbed the "death zone."

In marriage, there is a most perilous peak every man must overcome and a death zone to be vigorously avoided. And it has to do with communication, pride, and self-awareness.

THE FOOLISHNESS OF PRIDE

I'm convinced that the greatest contributor to communication dysfunction is pride. It's like an invasive species, which if not nipped in the bud, grows uncontrollably until it chokes out all other life. It starts when either a spouse refuses to admit fault or fails to see it; then it grows and morphs until it contaminates every conversation. C. S. Lewis wrote, "Pride is spiritual cancer: it eats up the very possibility of love, or contentment, or even common sense."[4]

Like a virus, strains of pride that survive only become more resistant to defeat. We must not only be watchful over pride, we must *hate* it. "The fear of the LORD is hatred of evil. Pride and arrogance and the way of evil" (Proverbs 8:13). If we fear God, we hate evil. And if we are to hate evil, we must despise arrogance and pride.

Let's look at how we as men uniquely struggle with pride and how it informs our communication.

Step one? We must know what we don't know.

---

4. C. S. Lewis, *Mere Christianity* (New York: HarperCollins, 1980), 126.

THE DUNNING-KRUGER EFFECT

Psychologists have long observed what's known as the Dunning-Kruger effect. Basically, it refers to our tendency to grossly overestimate our competence early in the learning process. We think we know more than we do, and our level of confidence is unjustified by our competence.

In a nutshell, the Dunning-Kruger effect is knowing enough to be dangerous. Consider the following diagram.

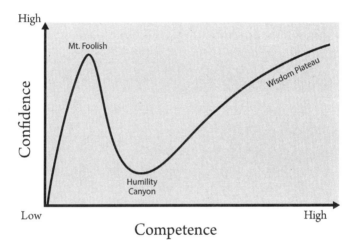

In every learning pursuit, one must begin the process somewhere. As a noob learns, his confidence outpaces his knowledge. Some have called the early peak on the graph Mount Stupid, but I prefer Mount Foolish, since only a fool would stay there. And biblically speaking, foolishness has more to do with lacking humility before God than IQ.

I've summited Mount Foolish plenty of times, and if you've ever learned anything new, so have you. According to the Dunning-Kruger effect, there's *always* an early peak, though some peaks are higher than others. Then, as learning continues—which is a *huge* key—every learner plummets into what I call Humility Canyon. This is where their confidence is proportionate to (or below) what they know. Then, over time, their confidence will grow proportionately as they learn until they master their craft. I've labeled this ideal place Wisdom Plateau.

SURVIVING MOUNT FOOLISH, CROSSING FOOL'S DIVIDE

As a man striving to love his wife well through how he communicates, the goal is to grow in communication competence *and* confidence *together*. To make that clear, I've added a diagonal line.

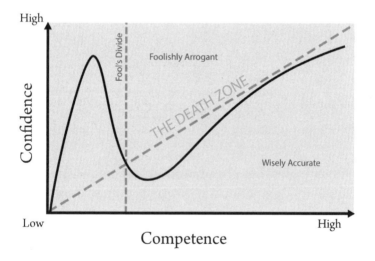

Everything above the diagonal is the death zone. Below the line is where life flourishes.

The key to surviving Mount Foolish is not camping on the summit. You must make the descent! And the faster the better.

It's as true for heart surgeons as it is for husbands. You don't want to stop learning ever, really, but especially not before you descend down the backside of Mount Foolish.

If you never complete the descent, it means your competence has stagnated and your confidence remains unmerited. Pride has arrested your development and your communication will suffer. Instead, you must make the descent *all the way* until you cross Fool's Divide. And, though you may spend most of your time south of the diagonal, there will likely be micropeaks that poke above it here and there. No husband is perfect in this regard. The most critical thing is that you keep learning, keep growing, keep changing, and never camp on a peak.

How do you know if you're camped out or not? Consider how pride may be at work in these contrasting statements:

CAMPING	DESCENDING
Unable to listen charitably	Hears wife's heart, responds to it
Will not admit when wrong	Confesses mistakes sincerely
Unwilling to actively improve communication	Committed to continued growth
Belittles based on knowledge	Never uses knowledge to make wife feel small
Invalidating and dismissive based on "facts"	Confirms meaning and seeks to understand
Avoids difficult conversations	Initiates whatever talks are necessary

The examples could go on, but the point is that if you lack humility in your communication life, it will stunt your growth and eventually starve your marriage. Your campsite on Mount

Foolish may have a great view, but death is imminent for those who stay.

The only way off the peak and out of the death zone is to make the descent into Humility Canyon. There it's warm. There, the beer flows like wine and humbled communicators instinctively flock like the salmon of Capistrano. Or, in case that reference goes unappreciated, it's a good place to be.

OUR BOASTWORTHY GOD

The key to growing in knowledge and confidence at the right pace is God-fearing humility. For this, we must turn to God's twofold Word (Scripture and Christ) to gain wisdom despite our inexperience. "The instruction of the LORD is perfect, renewing one's life; the testimony of the LORD is trustworthy, making the inexperienced wise" (Psalm 19:7 CSB). Heeding God's instruction renews life and turns communication greenhorns wise, but still, our boast is elsewhere. As Jeremiah wrote, "Let not the wise man boast in his wisdom... but let him who boasts boast in this, that he understands and knows me" (Jeremiah 9:23–24). Even having wisdom, which is a good thing, is not a worthy boast. (The surest litmus test for whether or not a man is a fool is if he brags of his wisdom.)

Instead, boast because you know God, because when you know God, you know Wisdom himself. And he's not one to leave you stranded in your pride and doomed to die. "Because of him you are in Christ Jesus, who *became to us* wisdom from God, righteousness and sanctification and redemption, so that, as it is written, 'Let the one who boasts, boast in the Lord'" (1 Corinthians 1:30–31, emphasis added).

> **KEY TAKEAWAY**
> Pride is like an invasive species, which if not nipped in the bud, grows uncontrollably until it chokes out all other life.

MEDIOCRITY VS MASTERY

Mediocrity	*Mastery*
Cannot recognize Mount Foolish	Quickly descends Mount Foolish
Comfortable camping in the death zone	Aims to reach Wisdom Plateau
Boasts in own wisdom	Boasts in Christ

APPLICATION QUESTIONS

Pride is sneaky and stealthy. How have you seen pride creep into your marital communication in the past? How did it affect the health of your marriage overall?

What are two or three ways you can guard your heart against arrogance in the future?

How can you ask your wife for help in this area? Be specific.

CHAPTER FOUR

THE INTEREST AND THE ANT
How Tiny Gains Compound into Massive Results

> *Go to the ant, O sluggard;*
> *consider her ways, and be wise.*
> *Without having any chief,*
> *officer, or ruler,*
> *she prepares her bread in summer*
> *and gathers her food in harvest.*
> Proverbs 6:6–8

If you take one thing away from this chapter, let it be this: *small communication gains matter.* In our years of ministry, I've seen too many men hit a tough spot in their marriage (sometimes it's one they got themselves into), so they set out to make things better. They'll binge listen to hours of podcast episodes, read marriage books, put their new knowledge into practice, then write in after a month telling me how they've tried it all and nothing is working. To them, my response is always the same: keep trying.

Keep going.

Keep doing what you know is right, even if the results aren't immediate.

Keep trusting God's Word.

Keep applying God's truth.

Keep loving your wife like your life depends on it, especially when she doesn't reciprocate.

Keep pleading with Christ to work miraculously in your marriage.

Keep expressing your devotion and desire for your wife, even if you feel like she can't hear it.

Just. Keep. Doing what's right.

Why? Because when it comes to realizing true, lasting change in your life, nothing compares to consistency over long lengths of time. And the reality is, that's usually the one thing those husbands have yet to try. Never underestimate the lasting change that comes from making small gains over sustained periods of time.

When speaking of honest business growth, my wise friend Jake often quips that the trick is "time plus pressure." It's how diamonds are made, and apparently it's how great businesses grow. I'll add, it's also how marital improvements are compounded.

Apply steady pressure, give it time, and watch things transform.

GO TO THE ANT

Consider this proverb, "Go to the ant, O sluggard; consider her ways, and be wise" (Proverbs 6:6). It's an odd proposition, but since creation groans with the glories of God, why shouldn't we find wisdom in an anthill? So, what is it about the ant that is particularly wise? Though her stature is slight, Solomon is inviting us to appreciate her consistency, diligence, and self-directedness.

The ant is a slow-burn worker. She is wise because she plods. She plays the long game, gathering food over weeks and months. With diligence and skill, she prepares her summer feast. Later in Proverbs we read, "The ants are a people not strong, yet they provide their food in the summer" (Proverbs 30:25). Ants aren't admired for their strength, but for their persistent diligence. Still need proof? Topple an anthill and come back tomorrow. It will either be rebuilt or well on its way.

I don't know a single husband who hasn't toppled a few proverbial anthills in his marriage. I know fewer husbands who were able to reconstruct them without persistent diligence. Wives will agree that feeling consistently, predictably loved is better than a sporadic grand gesture any day of the week.

SLOW STARTING, QUICKLY COMPOUNDING EFFECTS

The power of consistent communication habits isn't just that you'll pile up daily improvements, but rather that every improvement you make is *compounding*. To illustrate, I have a question.

Which would you rather have?

A) $1 million right now

B) $0.01 that doubles every day for a month

No cheating or calculators allowed. What would you choose?

If you chose option A, you'd be $1 million richer right now. Not bad! Congratulations, you're a millionaire! That is, until you pay the taxman. But still, you should be able to buy a house outright.

But as these illustrations predictably go, the better answer is the less obvious one.

If you chose option B, you'd only have $0.01 today, but by the end of the month you'd have $10.6 million. Not a bad trade! Skip $1 million now for $10 million in 31 days. It's easy to see the upside from the finish line, but the beginning would be dicey.

Even with a 100 percent daily compound interest rate, the initial gains with option B are tiny. On day 15, you'd only have $163. It isn't until day 18 that you break the $1,000 mark, but just ten days later you're in the millions. As with any compounding interest chart, the tiniest increases are early but the graph gets steeper the longer you go.

The same is true in your communication habits. As with anything new, it will take upfront work that will feel unfruitful and unnatural at times. Your early gains may be discouraging, but take heart and look to the ant. Every tiny gain you make is compounding, and you need not start with much to see mountainous growth over time.

I must admit, the 100 percent compounding rate helps make the point, but it's not realistic in most scenarios. Let's look at 1 percent.

THE 1 PERCENT EFFECT

What would it look like if you were to communicate 1 percent better today than you did yesterday? Think of a few small changes you might make. Whatever you do, improving by 1 percent is feasible and won't seem like a lot of effort. But, if repeated daily, the improvement gets massive. Keep it up for a year and you'll be floored.

Best-selling author and habits guru James Clear writes,

> [I]mproving by 1 percent isn't particularly notable—sometimes it isn't even noticeable—but

it can be far more meaningful, especially in the long run. The difference a tiny improvement can make over time is astounding. Here's how the math works out: if you can get 1 percent better each day for one year, you'll end up thirty-seven times better by the time you're done. Conversely, if you get 1 percent worse each day for one year, you'll decline nearly down to zero. What starts as a small win or a minor setback accumulates into something much more.[5]

Thirty-seven times better *after just the first year.* Think of how much better your marriage will be! And I'm not talking about writing multipage love letters or spending hours in deep conversation every day. I'm talking about small, intentional, incremental improvements day after day that will lead to truly outstanding results. I'm talking about…

taking an extra five seconds to think before you respond.

asking a thoughtful question you've never thought to ask before.

initiating a conversation when you'd rather remain silent.

taking note of your heart posture when you fall into patterns of critical speech.

offering a genuine word of encouragement out of the blue.

beholding new opportunities to love your wife through your words.

Sounds doable, right? It is, and that's the good news. Without a doubt, you can do this. But there's sobering news as well:

---

5. James Clear, *Atomic Habits* (New York: Penguin Random House, 2018), 15.

only you can do this. And, if you don't, much is at stake. Your communication will not improve if you don't set out to improve it. But, if you do, there is much to be gained.

Depending on your circumstances and marital dynamic, your efforts could produce quick returns or they could yield near-zero results. If the latter is the case, take heart. Look to the ant. Apply steady pressure over a long period of time and let the diamond crystallize as it will. After all, you're not in this for immediate returns, you're in this for life. And you're in this for the good of your wife and the eternal glory of Christ.

> **KEY TAKEAWAY**
> Every tiny gain you make is compounding, and you need not start with much to see mountainous growth over time.

MEDIOCRITY VS MASTERY

Mediocrity	*Mastery*
Tries to improve but fizzles out if results aren't quick enough	Understands that true growth takes effort, time, and patience
Values grand gestures more than consistent growth	Favors consistency with grand gestures thrown in
Lets discouragement snuff out efforts	Remembers his purpose especially during seasons of discouragement

APPLICATION QUESTIONS

Think about the habits you have cultivated as a husband. What good communication habits do you already have? What bad habits have you formed? List two or three of each.

What are a few small habits you can start building immediately that will lead to the greatest results over time? If you're stumped, consider the list of ideas mentioned in the chapter.

What is one new communication habit that will make your wife feel especially loved?

CHAPTER FIVE

THE KILT AND THE CLAYMORE
Disarming (and Disrobing) Defenses to Restore Marital Eden

> *She took of its fruit and ate, and she also gave some to her husband who was with her, and he ate. Then the eyes of both were opened, and they knew that they were naked. And they sewed fig leaves together and made themselves loincloths. And they heard the sound of the* L ORD *God walking in the garden in the cool of the day, and the man and his wife hid themselves from the presence of the* L ORD *God among the trees of the garden.*
> Genesis 3:6–8

We often recommend that married couples fight naked during seasons of conflict. It's mostly a metaphor, though applying our advice literally has been known to have certain advantages. The metaphor is intended to help couples be more vulnerable with each other. Coincidentally, as I've discovered, vulnerable is exactly how it feels to be literally caught on a battlefield naked like I was. Well, sort of.

It was a brisk Friday morning, and I found myself browsing bolts of fabric at a Michael's somewhere in the outskirts of Seattle. I'm no seamster, so this was strange. A few buddies and I were looking for material and ideas for our costumes for a community viewing of *Braveheart*. But this wasn't just a friendly get-together. We were headed into war.

For part of college, I lived in what's best described as a Christian fraternity. Just trade the jocks and parties for church kids and chapels, and you're 90 percent there. We weren't part of the Greek system, but our house was smack-dab in the middle of the thriving Greek Row at the University of Washington. It was definitely an "in the world but not of it" sort of situation, and I loved every minute.

That fateful Friday at the fabric store marked the last days of our house's annual "Week of Man." It was a glorious tradition where, for seven days, the young men of the University Christian Union completed mostly stupid challenges in order to accumulate "man points" in hopes of being crowned man-champion of the week. It was all a big joke and the challenges weren't meant to be taken too seriously.

For example, if you asked for a girl's phone number, you got a point. Get another point if she says yes; two points for a rejection. You'd also get points for other stereotypically manly tasks like lifting heavy things, not showering for the week, or eating dinner with your shirt off—you know, "manly" stuff.

Then there was the grand finale.

On Saturday night—during peak party hours on Greek Row—all twenty-something of us guys would cram onto our faux leather couches in the basement and watch the manliest movie of all time, *Braveheart*. Except, this wasn't your average viewing, and it was the reason I was in the fabric store the day before.

In preparation for the movie, each man in the house was challenged to craft their best Scottish battle garb and brandish the most epic weapon they could forge. Of course, William Wallace face paint was a given.

Then, right in the middle of the movie, before the biggest battle—with regalia and armament and all—we'd pause the show and race down Greek Row, sprinting through the Saturday night party-going masses, wielding our warcrafts and screaming at the tops of our lungs, "Freedom!"

That was the plan, anyway. Back to the fabric store.

I hadn't made a ton of points throughout the week, and *Braveheart* was my chance to clinch a win, so I went all out on my outfit. Fortuitously, I found some blue and green tartan fabric, so I bought a few yards—just enough to wrap around my waist with a little extra to cut a strip for a sash. My kilt was complete, now to forge a weapon.

If a big sword is good, an eight-foot sword is awesome, so that's exactly what I made. The house forge was out of commission, so I made do with a baseball bat, a stick, cardboard, duct tape, and silver spray paint. By the time it was done, my sword looked like something out of Final Fantasy VII. Together, my outfit was a masterpiece; my pièce de résistance.

Let the movie roll!

ONTO THE BATTLEFIELD

As a pro tip, when you wear a makeshift kilt to earn pretend man points during the made-up Week of Man, you must do so authentically. And, according to every source I could find, that means keeping your bits and bobs free and breezy in the nethers. Underwear is not only unnecessary, it's a party foul. So, since I couldn't risk losing points on a night as monumental as this, I obliged.

This is where the fighting naked analogy comes in.

For all my academic advances, sewing was not a subject in which I excelled. This became crystal clear during the intermission when we took to the streets. I remember it like it was yesterday. We hit pause on the film. It's as if time warped into slow motion. We emerged from the basement steps, out into the crisp ruckus of Saturday night. I raised my mighty sword, and belted out "Freedom!" with full gusto.

Which reminds me. Speaking of belts…

One more pro tip: three safety pins are no replacement for a sturdy leather belt.

Oh no, I thought.

Only a few strides in, I was horrified.

However much fabric I bought, it wasn't enough. I mean, it was "enough," but it wasn't *enough*. At least not to go sprinting down Frat Row on a Friday night. There I was, barely covered in two yards of paper-thin fabric, running down the busiest stretch of Seattle sidewalk, surrounded by scores of gawking, drunk coeds, and brandishing a mainsail-sized sword with the aerodynamics of a mattress box. Every step was a gamble, and I was playing for keeps. With one hand I wielded my sword high overhead, with the other, I desperately held onto my kilt. And my dignity.

Thankfully, I can say that I and my motley band of freedom fighters made it around the block, up the alley, and back to the house without besmirching my good name. I can also say I learned a few valuable lessons that day, which I'll happily share with you in the name of better marital communication.

BROKEN UTOPIA AND INNOCENCE RESTORED

There's a special vulnerability that happens when you're naked, and not just physically. Of course, disrobing at home *can* be a great option for married folks looking to work through minor communication issues, but mostly I'm talking about emotional and spiritual nakedness. I'm talking about *innocence*.

The passage at this chapter's outset describes that fateful day in the garden when Adam and Eve ate of the tree. After eating, "the eyes of both were opened, and they knew that they were naked… and the man and his wife hid themselves from the presence of the Lord God among the trees of the garden" (Genesis 3:6–8). Just a few verses earlier they had been naked and unashamed. That was over. They broke utopia and they felt it in their guts. So they hid.

In a similar sense, we feel our own nakedness and the vulnerability that goes along with it. Deep down, we are keenly aware of our flaws and faults and our need to hide. When Adam and Eve hid in the trees, God called them out of hiding and, in their nakedness and shame, he covered them. They tried to cover themselves with fig leaves—my makeshift kilt comes to mind— but it was insufficient. So, God clothed them in animal skins (Genesis 3:21). An animal died—a sacrifice was made—that they might be covered by God.

You and I have the cosmic privilege of seeing Eden set squarely in the shadow of the cross. We can see now what it all would eventually mean. From here, we know what God's covering would eventually look like, we know how his voice calling sinners back to him would eventually sound, and we've seen the cruciform tree behind which the offenders of God would ultimately hide.

When God forgives, he restores innocence. Not naiveté, but *legal* innocence. Your offense has been cleared and your record expunged. Not only that but he has called you his son. This is the basis of fighting naked in marriage.

LOIN CLOTHS LOST

One of the unique aspects of a marriage between two regenerate hearts is that there are opportunities to return to Eden-like innocence and vulnerability within the covenant. When you're naked with your wife—whether it's physically, emotionally, or spiritually—you need not feel shame. It's idyllic and true but not always our experience. Why?

As life wears on and you fall into routines, it's easy to let your hearts grow obscured toward one another. It's a gradual drift that results in communication habits that are tough to break. And, if poor communication patterns persist, conflict is inevitable. Then, instead of working through it with patience and vulnerability, you grab your armor and prepare for war. But what if you didn't? What if instead, you threw the armor aside, cast down your loin cloth, and fought naked? There are at least three clear advantages to be gained if you do.

1. *Lowered weapons.*

It's all too easy to weaponize our words with those we love most. We know the sharpest words to cut the deepest and we intuitively practice pitch-perfect tones for delivering decisive blows. This is usually the result of familiarity and failed communication boundaries coupled with deep hurts or brewing bitterness. But it doesn't have to be so.

So, what if you led your wife by putting down your weapons? Lowering your guard? Nothing defuses a tense situation quicker than laying down your weapons.

2. Lowered defenses.

Going into battle without armor is a death wish. In marriage, it's a vote of confidence. Not getting defensive doesn't mean you're defenseless; it means Christ is your defender, not you. And, if you're in the wrong, you have only holiness to gain by being corrected! With those realizations in mind, you need not assume a posture of defensiveness. If your wife attacks you, instead of returning fire with a snappy defense, you're freed to hear her heart despite her words, to seek understanding, and to respond in love.

3. No surprise attacks.

I'm amazed at how couples (us included) manipulate each other so naturally and unwittingly. There's a strong human tendency to want to be right at any cost. So, one of the best ways you can fight naked is by identifying the common manipulation tactics in your communication and refusing to use them.

It's impossible to hide a trick up your sleeve when you have no sleeves.

A RETURN TO EDEN?

You and your wife will never be perfect on this side of glory. Eden rests in the shadow of the cross, but the light of Christ's return is yet to come. Still, you can grow. And still, your marriage can be a safe, Eden-like space where you exercise grace and love unlike in any other human relationship.

It will take work, intentionality, and a fair bit of nakedness. But thankfully, you have the cover of your covenant and full assurance of the gospel, which beats a tattered kilt on a crowded sidewalk every time.

> **KEY TAKEAWAY**
> Marriage between two regenerate hearts provides opportunities to return to Eden-like innocence and vulnerability within the covenant.

MEDIOCRITY VS MASTERY

Mediocrity	Mastery
Weaponizes words to defeat	Lays down arms
Gets and stays defensive	Lowers defenses; open to correction if needed
Mounts surprise attacks to gain advantage	Mindful of manipulation tendencies, seeks to avoid them

APPLICATION QUESTIONS

It's a human tendency to get defensive during conflict. What are your most prominent defense tactics during conflict with your wife? Consider the ways you listen, engage, speak, or refuse to do either.

Think of your most recent argument. How could it have started (and ended) differently if you had lowered your defenses and discarded your weapons? In other words, what might have happened if you had fought naked as explained in this chapter?

What is one practical way you can fight naked in the future? Be specific (and not just literal).

CHAPTER SIX

THE FOG AND THE FRIENDLY FIRE
You Have an Enemy, and It's Not Your Wife

Then the LORD God said, "It is not good that the man should be alone; I will make him a helper fit for him."
Genesis 2:18

Barring amateur paintball competitions, I've never fought in battle. But I know men who have. Their stories will curl your toes. War is terrifying and disorienting. Messy and unclear. So much so that analysts call this disorientation or uncertainty the *fog of war*. It's a phrase popularized to refer to the imprecision inherent to military operations, both tactically and strategically.

Strategically, decisions made before or during battle are rarely precise or perfect. They're clouded by unknown variables, unpredictable circumstances, and the inability to control outcomes. Tactically, soldiers experience disorientation of direction, confusion around orders and their execution, fear, doubt, gunfire, weather, and other variables which all contribute to the fog of war. And it's a real problem. Fog of war is the leading cause of friendly fire.

Military analysts say there is no way to avoid the fog entirely. So, commanders must make do. They trade certainty for speed and precision for agility, all the while depending on the training and judgment of men in the field to just make things work. This is starting to sound a little like marriage. And it is.

THE FOG OF COMMUNICATION WAR

You can't predict everything you will face. Mistakes happen, circumstances explode, or your connection erodes. Some marital fog is unavoidable, but handling it poorly isn't.

To be clear, marriage is *not* war. Your marriage is a divine institution graciously given by God so you and your children might flourish, grow, and glorify him. Your union is a divinely architected cathedral that radiates the majesty of its heavenly Designer. Your only task is to step in and occupy God's masterfully crafted cathedral with obedience, joy, and faithfulness.

Still, as any married person will tell you, there are times when marriage *feels* less like a cathedral and more like a battlefield. Like battle, marriage can get messy, uncertain, and imprecise. At times, you will find yourself weighing precision against expedience and agility against accuracy. The trouble is, just as in the fog of war, the fog of *communication* war in marriage can lead to friendly fire. In a Christian marriage, this ought not be so.

IDENTIFY WHO THE ENEMY *ISN'T*

The first strategic reminder to avoid friendly fire amid the marital fog of war is to know your enemy. Here's an obvious clue:

It's not your wife. I'll repeat it one more time for those sitting in the back: Your wife is *not* your enemy! It must be repeated because "your spouse is not your enemy" is one of those truisms that everyone agrees with until they don't.

That's how the fog of war works. Things are simple until they're not. Clear until obfuscated. It's obvious that your wife isn't your enemy until the naggy-tone flak cannons destroy your recon flights and a "you're just like your father" landmine obliterates your emotional legs beneath the knees. Communication battle gets ugly and disorienting. You need crystal clarity in the trenches about who your fellow fighters are and what your shared objective is. When the terrible-timing-and-tone cannon smoke bellows through your bunker, it's too easy to forget.

The foundational fact to keep in mind is, even in the heat of communication battle, your wife is designed specifically by God to be your helper, not your hinderer. She's an asset, not a liability. And to a marvelous degree.

SORELY NEEDED, DIVINELY DESIGNED, CAREFULLY FIT

In the creation account, God made and commissioned Adam to work the garden, but something—*someone*—was noticeably missing. So God said, "It is not good that the man should be alone; I will make him a helper fit for him" (Genesis 2:18).

Consider three observations from that text:

1) It's not good for man to be alone.
2) So God made him a helper.
3) And that helper was *fit* for man.

As Eve was given to Adam, so was your wife given to you. You needed her, God gave her to you, and she is your *fitted* helper.

Now, contrast the observations from Genesis 2:18 with how you communicate during wartime. Do you speak to your wife as the God-designed, custom-fit helper that she is? Or do you talk to her like she's an enemy combatant, airdropped behind your defenses to usurp your authority and upend your sovereign self-nation? The key to eschewing the fog in your wartime communication is knowing with full certainty that your wife is your divinely designed, appointed, and fit helper.

I'll say it again, your wife is not your enemy.

THE TRUE COMMUNICATION COMBATANTS

To be sure, your marriage *does* have enemies; it's just that your wife isn't one of them. You are co-commandos fighting toward a common objective and against shared enemies. Let's identify a few of them so you can take them out with surgical precision.

The Enemy Proper

You have an enemy who would love to see your marriage fail: the devil. He's a prowler (1 Peter 5:8), a liar (John 8:44), and a tempter (Matthew 4, 1 Thessalonians 3:5). Be the protector your marriage needs; do as Peter commends, "Be sober-minded; be watchful" (1 Peter 5:8). And as Paul exhorts, "Take up the shield of faith, with which you can extinguish all the flaming darts of the evil one" (Ephesians 6:16).

The devil is your enemy. Defeat *him*, not your wife.

Your Flesh

In Christ, your salvation is sure and your sanctification is in progress. James writes, "What causes quarrels and what causes fights among you? Is it not this, that your passions are at war within you?" (James 4:1). You're still at war with your flesh, and both you and your wife are capable of communication double agency. Know which side you're both on.

Your flesh is your enemy. Mortify *it*, not your wife.

Miscommunication

Much is said in this book about clarifying communication, but I mention miscommunication here to highlight its enemy status. Solomon writes, "An unreliable messenger stumbles into trouble, but a reliable messenger brings healing" (Proverbs 13:17). Both you and your wife have the capacity to be unreliable messengers. Work together to increase the reliability of your communication instead of fixating on killing whoever happens to be the messenger. Healing will ensue.

Miscommunication is your enemy. Snuff *it*, not your wife.

Habits and Ruts

The final enemies I'll highlight are bad communication habits and unhelpful ruts. Knee-jerk reactions are rarely the best options and default tones drift toward contempt faster than kindness. Build awareness of habits and ruts that destroy healthy dialogue, then eradicate them like the vermin they are.

Habits and ruts are your enemy. Avoid *them* like the plague, not your wife.

AGGRESSIVELY OFFENSIVE

You need tactics to identify and defend against enemies, but a good offense is invaluable in securing lasting victory. You must advance the line and conquer new territories, or ongoing war is inevitable. Who wants to live in a constant state of conflict? The best way to secure ongoing victory—and *peace*—in your communication is to go on the offensive.

Here are a few starter objectives to overtake.

Build Shared Vernacular

Do you have shared language during conflict? What sorts of words and notions are free to flow in your marriage? What communication culture are you building? How will you process external circumstances, in-laws, the news, or whatever else comes up? And how will you address sin in a productive manner? Much of this probably sounds basic, and it is, but more victories are secured by blocking and tackling than by hurling Hail Marys.

This is covered in greater detail in chapter 11.

Target Communication

Knowing your shared objective, you each need good targeting systems. Lazily aimed words veer off target and result in friendly fire. Be careful to speak and hear with 3,000-yard accuracy. Couples who talk past one another are either very bad at aiming their words, or they're always moving the targets. More on that in the next chapter.

Love your bride by aiming your words carefully, but also lead her by gently helping her aim hers. In the event of friendly fire, this will require thick skin. Still, you're the man for the job.

Delineate Sides

The quickest way we've discovered to clear the fog of war is to clearly and decisively delineate sides. If we're alert, either Selena or I will hit pause and interject, "I love you and I'm for us." Done genuinely, this interruption can pluck us up from our opposing sides and place us shoulder to shoulder so we can fight alongside each other once again. In the same spirit, you can remind her that your shared goal in the current dialogue is to gain understanding, seek reconciliation, find resolution, and ultimately, experience mutual sanctification. Then, you can both breathe deep and continue on.

God knows you and he knows your wife. He knows the various battles you will face. He also knows exactly what you need so he gave you your exact wife. Remind yourself of that and be sure she knows this with zero doubt: she is not your enemy, the issue is. Then, fight *for* her and *beside* her with everything you've got.

> **KEY TAKEAWAY**
> You and your wife are co-commandos fighting toward a common objective and against shared enemies.

MEDIOCRITY VS MASTERY

Mediocrity	*Mastery*
Hasty to blame and attack wife during conflict	Sees wife as his fit helper, not the enemy
Prone to friendly fire through poorly chosen words and deficient targeting	Bridles the tongue
Unwilling or unable to engage the true enemies in the conflict	Soberly discerns and engages the true enemy in each conflict

APPLICATION QUESTIONS

What does it mean that your wife is not your enemy? In the space below, write two or three statements that start with, "My wife is my…" Briefly describe why each statement is true.

Oftentimes, our first reactions are the most telling. What is your go-to, knee-jerk response to your wife during conflict? Why do you think you respond that way?

How can you and your wife work together to defeat each of the enemies identified in this chapter? Be specific.

The Enemy Proper

Your Flesh

Miscommunication

Habits and Ruts

CHAPTER SEVEN

THE GOALPOSTS AND THE GASLIGHT
The Scandalous Subtlety of Manipulation

> For there is no distinction:
> for all have sinned and fall short of the glory of God,
> and are justified by his grace as a gift, through the
> redemption that is in Christ Jesus.
> Romans 3:22–24

Manipulation is a gangly sin. It's a lie that lies about being a lie. When it's present in marriage, it is subtle, silent, and makes no sudden moves. It's covert and hidden, camouflaged by its familiarity. Victims of manipulation struggle to see the lies, and, as I'll posit, manipulators themselves are often clueless of how creatively they've learned to bend the truth.

Psychologists define manipulation as a form of emotional abuse aimed at controlling the other person. I would add, "by bending, twisting, and mischaracterizing the truth into a lie."

I'll get into various styles of manipulation in relationships, but first I need to ask: Are you a manipulator in your marriage? For most, the first reaction is no. It's natural to think, *There's no way I'm the manipulator.* Based on the definition, who wants to be called controlling and abusive? They're heavy words, but hear me out.

In our years teaching on marriage and working with couples, nothing has surprised quite like the revelation that everyone is capable of manipulation. Every husband and every wife. How? Because manipulation is gangly and sneaky and shy. As we've found, it's all too easy for its subtle forms to creep into even the healthiest marriages.

THE BAD NEWS IS BAD, BUT THE GOOD NEWS IS BETTER

Before you blame me for being pessimistic, consider the passage at the start of this chapter: "All have sinned and fall short of the glory of God" (Romans 3:23). *All* includes you and me. Not only that, we're sinners capable of complete rebellion against God. Even the good things we manage to do are "like filthy rags" when compared to the holiness of God (Isaiah 64:6 NIV). This means that even the most well-meaning husbands are capable of emotionally manipulating and seeking to control their wives. Again, this includes you and me.

Why do I share this? Confronting your ability to sin in worse ways than you realize will either crush you or cast you headlong into the grace of God. You'll die under its load or retreat into God's chest. Thank God Paul didn't end the book of Romans there. Instead, he went on, saying those same sinners "are justified by his grace as a gift, through the redemption that is in Christ

Jesus" (Romans 3:24). The bad news is bad, but the good news is better.

The bad news is that you're capable of egregious sin (v. 23), but the good news is that Christ has saved you from the bondage of sin and is calling you to walk in his righteousness (v. 24). This goes for both you and your wife, and you both need the same grace available in Christ! My prayer is that by learning about your own manipulation habits, you can root them out and walk in new levels of truth and love.

COMMON MANIPULATION TACTICS

Consider the common manipulation tactics below and honestly assess your communication habits with your wife (try to focus on yourself, *not* your wife). Do any of these sound familiar?

Triangulation

This kind of manipulation happens when, in order to make a case, one spouse cites friends, coworkers, or other biased references to add credibility and social pressure favoring their side of an issue. Examples include one spouse saying something like, "Everyone thinks that…" or, as a husband might say, "Steve's wife lets him go out with the guys; why won't you?" Or a wife could argue, "Paul took his family to Maui last year, so why can't we go?"

The triangulator has their objective in clear view, so they'll build a case by including carefully curated assenting opinions from friends and others in order to make the other feel like they're on the wrong side of the issue.

Have you ever triangulated to win an argument?

Moving the Goalposts

This tactic is a logical fallacy that changes the rules of the discourse by demanding greater or different evidence in order for the other person to refute a claim. It's similar to changing subjects in that it displaces the basis of the conversation and confuses the efforts of the other.

This tactic also includes blaming your spouse for something, making demands to alleviate your frustration, then upping the demands once they've been met.

Imagine a husband who spends his non-working hours playing video games away from the family. Frustrated, his wife voices her concerns, to which he responds, "You never seem like you want to talk." After weeks of her attempting to start conversations, he still spends just as much time gaming. When she confronts him again, he either says she didn't try hard enough, he didn't know, or he creates some other reason or way for her to fix it. The goalposts have moved, and the wife feels more hopeless than ever.

Have you ever moved the goalposts?

Gaslighting

Gaslighters invalidate individuals and arguments by making the other person question their memory, identity, or reality itself. By persistently questioning and rewriting history, the gaslighter gains power in the relationship because the other person's confidence has been undermined so thoroughly that they no longer trust their intuition or judgment.

Key gaslighting phrases include, "You're overreacting," "You're imagining things," "I never said that," "It's not a big deal," or "I only did that because I love you." Gaslighters will often have very selective memories and will weaponize trust and privacy to isolate others from objective community.

Gaslighting comes in subtle and overt forms and those who do it may or may not be aware that they're doing it. This form of manipulation is especially harmful because it erodes trust and confidence while enthroning one spouse as the arbiter of reality in the relationship. Gaslighters are frequently narcissists.

Are you a gaslighter?

Dismissiveness

A dismissive spouse will seek to undercut the other person's assertions or accomplishments by invalidating them or through disingenuous argumentation. The main issue with dismissiveness is that it doesn't allow the main source of contention enough time or space to be worked through fully.

Examples include telling your wife she's just upset because she's hungry or tired, or nitpicking an argument and invalidating it because a word was used imprecisely or incorrectly.

Are you dismissive toward your wife?

Projection

Projection is when one person attributes their own feelings or desires to the other person as a means of masking or distracting from their own similar feelings.

Examples include one spouse blaming the other for being too worried about money when they're the one who is typically first to fear lack, or the habitually critical wife who constantly feels judged by her friends. Another example is a husband who obsesses about his wife's faithfulness—which can materialize as jealousy or distrust—while he secretly uses pornography and frequently flirts with women at work.

Projecting one's own negative traits onto the other is a psychological defense mechanism where the person doing the projecting shifts focus and therefore, blame, to the other person as a means of making themselves feel better.

Do you project your own negative traits onto your wife?

Treating Like a Child

This is actually a subcategory of gaslighting that specifically makes the other person question their own intellect or doubt their ability to handle responsibility. By treating the other person like a child—often using patronizing, sarcastic, or condescending language—the manipulator convinces their spouse to "let them handle" whatever situation is in question.

Examples include throwing past divisions of labor in the other's face, like, "You can't even balance the checkbook, how could you possibly know what our budget is?"

In general, this is a form of talking down to the other person that causes them to doubt their abilities and instead default to dependence or codependence on the manipulator.

Do you treat your wife like a child?

The Silent Treatment

The name says it all. While some time of quietness is healthy and natural to help a husband or wife process their thoughts and feelings, the silent treatment is a weaponized version of this.

A spouse who uses the silent treatment cuts off communication in order to punish their spouse during or after a conflict. The connection-starved spouse eventually "breaks" by conceding their side of the argument in order to reinstate the relationship and experience peace once again.

Do you give your wife the silent treatment?

LIES UN-MASKED AND UN-MASTERED

Upon first review, I was personally shocked and convicted by the number of subtle and not-so-subtle manipulation habits I had deployed over the years. The question is, Do any of these sound familiar to you? And, as a husband, what should you do about them? Here are four tangible steps to take to root out manipulation in your communication. The following application questions will guide you further.

1. Recognize

You can't begin to make progress until you have an accurate diagnosis. My hope is that this chapter helped you understand how a few manipulation tactics could function in a marriage. But recognition can't start and end with you. Blind spots are far too difficult to self-diagnose. You need God, your wife, and godly men to help. Ask them what they see in you and (this is the hard part) trust them to be honest and loving. Then, move on to the next step.

2. Repent

Once you recognize and take responsibility for your tendencies and faults in this area, confess them to God, ask for forgiveness, and turn toward righteousness. He stands ready to forgive, love, and teach you to walk in step with the Holy Spirit.

3. Reconcile

When I approached Selena and articulated how I thought I had used manipulation tactics in our marriage, the change in her expression and manner was palpable. She felt seen and she expressed her gratitude. I asked for her forgiveness, then I asked for her help. She graciously agreed and went on to confess some of her own manipulation tendencies to me. Reconciliation is a miraculous, beautiful process.

4. Remove

Once the tactics are exposed and confessed, you can now have a standing agreement to help one another keep your communication clear of manipulative tendencies. It's a challenge to call them out lovingly in the heat of an argument, but at least you're speaking a shared language, having identified a common enemy.

Manipulation is a sneaky, quiet intruder into otherwise healthy marriages. And, if a marriage is unhealthy, it will only serve to deepen the dysfunction. Still, fellow husband, be vigilant. Fight for the entire truth, complete transparency, and consistent honesty in your communication. Strive to eradicate manipulation from your marriage, and flourish alongside your bride in the full light of the truth.

> **KEY TAKEAWAY**
>
> By learning about your own manipulation habits, you can root them out and walk in new levels of truth and love.

MEDIOCRITY VS MASTERY

Mediocrity	*Mastery*
Uses manipulation tactics (knowingly or not) for selfish gain	Seeks to eradicate manipulation tactics from all communication
Doesn't ask for help in revealing blind spots	Earnestly asks God, wife, and other men to help identify manipulative tendencies
Refuses to admit when manipulating; won't repent	Recognizes and repents of manipulation

APPLICATION QUESTIONS

As you read through the common manipulation tactics above, did any feel close to home? If so, which ones? If none, draw a pretty picture in the space below.

Take an honest inventory of your last few arguments with your wife. Did you deploy any manipulation tactics? Write them down along with any "trigger" phrases that help you identify them.

CHAPTER EIGHT

THE TINDER AND THE STORM
The Particulars of Communication Forestry

So also the tongue is a small member,
yet it boasts of great things.
How great a forest is set ablaze by such a small fire!
And the tongue is a fire, a world of unrighteousness.
The tongue is set among our members, staining the
whole body, setting on fire the entire course of life,
and set on fire by hell.
James 3:5–6

Early in my career I worked for the Department of Natural Resources in our home state of Washington. The agency is charged with stewarding hundreds of thousands of forested acres, which includes wildfire response. I was a desk jockey and my job was great, but the heroes of the agency were those in the field. Foresters were our rockstars and firefighters our elite army. Thanks to my job, I got to work closely with many of them.

There's a Hemingwayness about people in forestry. The mustachioed Ron Swanson caricature of a government-employed, woodworking mountain man isn't far off. In my travels, I marveled at the rugged, matter-of-fact nature of the men and women working in and among the trees. And I wondered what it might be like to trade my khakis and computer for a Pulaski and a pair of boots.

Then, one day I got the chance.

Though a desk rider, I was still a DNR man. This meant I had the chance to be deployed as a "single resource" during particularly intense wildfires. Training included. So, I signed up.

I learned all about wildland fires, safety, and tactics to quench wildfire at massive scales. What struck me most was how rapidly a fire could grow out of control. There are countless factors at play, but three of the biggest contributors to wildfire gone wild are an accumulation of tinder, consistently dry conditions, and an inciting event (such as lightning or a poorly quenched campfire). All three of these major variables are necessary for runaway wildfire. Take one away and the fire's out in time for supper.

Your marriage is the forest and your tongue is a fire. And, just like a rampant wildfire, reaching communication scorched-earth at home only happens with all three factors in play: tinder, drought, and an incitement. We'll explore each one next, but first, to the Word (and the tongue).

A TONGUE AMOK OR A FIRE CONTAINED

The Word of God makes clear the power of the words of humans. Through words souls know souls and man knows God. By his words God creates and by our words we build and destroy, bless and curse. In his letter to the early saints, James warned, "The tongue is fire, a world of unrighteousness" (James 3:6). Later he wrote, "No human being can tame the tongue. It is a restless evil, full of deadly poison" (James 3:8). Can a warning get any clearer? According to James, the tongue is fire, a world of unrighteousness, untamable, a restless evil. It's *injurious, pernicious*, and on a more garden-variety note, *dangerous*.

The tongue is fire.

How can a husband expect to flourish in his marital communication forest if the words and ways he speaks are misaligned with biblical love? He shouldn't. His unbridled tongue will torch it all. It's the Molotov cocktail to his connubial kindling pile.

Or it can be something else. Something safer. Still fire, yes, but not the kind that burns.

Just as a safely contained campfire provides warmth and a means for a hot meal, so might the tongue, when wielded with love, be a source of blessing to your wife when you speak.

THE THREE WILDFIRE FACTORS

Using your words wisely and lovingly is the first line of defense in protecting your marriage from communication wildfires. Is your tongue sparking wildfires or hearth fires? If wildfires, it will prove helpful to understand the three factors that let communication wildfires burn amok. Let's explore each one below.

Factor 1: Drought

My communication dynamics with God affect the communication dynamics with my wife. When I'm not spending adequate time in God's Word, when I've not been disciplined in my prayer life, and when I'm operating in my own strength—not walking in the Spirit—my heart grows anxious and dry. In turn, my angst works its way to my wife via snappy tones and emotional reclusion. My default settings are not to open up outward, but to fold inward. To shrivel.

The solution? Stay watered. Christ said that the water he gives—himself—will become "a spring of water welling up to eternal life," and that those who drink it "will never be thirsty again" (John 4:13–14). Water quenches thirst and wildfire alike.

What's the communication climate in your marriage? Is it dried out and prone to wildfire? Or is it saturated with the living water that wells up into eternal life? Bear in mind, there is no substitute. No book replaces *the* Book. And no words replace *the* Word. Podcasts are great, and YouTube has helped me fix my car more than once, but neither can ever feed my soul like the Word of God. If you want your life and marriage to thrive, you must go to the source of life himself and drink deep of the water only he provides.

Factor 2: Tinder

Along with dry conditions, collected tinder along the forest floor accelerates wildfire mayhem. When lightning strikes or a campfire is left to smolder, nearby fuel is the difference between a non-event and FEMA intervention.

As for marital communication, tinder includes every unresolved frustration, conflict, and issue. It's the gradual piling up of every unsettled pang and spasm of life, composting slowly, exothermically, on the forest floor of your union.

Consider, what sort of tinder are you prone to gather? Could it be the frustration you felt when your wife was too tired for intimacy? Maybe it's the irritation your wife feels when you're home late from work for the third time in a week, or the bitterness brewing because your parents lack tact? Or perhaps it's that the kids have been acting up and the puppy tidily eviscerated yet another one of your shoes?

Whatever your tinder, you know it well. As the husband, being aware of its accumulation and effects is one of your greatest opportunities to improve communication. Address the buildup on your forest floor, talk through tough things, and give your bride an opportunity to process storms before lightning strikes, which is what we'll cover next.

Factor 3: Incitement

This is the final piece that makes for communication wildfire: the *inciting event*. No wildfire ignites spontaneously; there's always something that sets it off. Lightning strikes are common. As are stray cigarettes and sadly quenched campfires. Meth labs and moonshiners too. These events are sometimes preventable—as is the case if your tongue set the blaze—but not always.

Life is unpredictable like lightning. We have far less control than we think. One morning it's life as usual and by evening, your world is inside-out. Maybe your transmission blows up (been there) or you discover black mold in one of your closet walls (been there too). Or worse, you get injured in an accident or receive a cancer diagnosis.

Sin incites wildfire as well. A husband or wife gets caught in sin and trust is shattered. Or someone outside your marriage sins against you: criminals burglarize your home, your wife's best friend gossips behind her back, your boss throws you under the bus, or a beloved pastor has a moral failure. Who sees this stuff coming?

The point is, life is packed with uncertainty, and inciting events strike when they want, not when convenient. Have you ever wondered why some people are more prone to drama than others? Small events can ignite big fires for some couples, while other couples seem impervious to the toughest storm. Why is that? It's probably something to do with factors one and two.

MANAGE ONE, MITIGATE ALL

In our years working with couples, the most devastating wildfires happen when they have dried out spiritually, let tinder piles grow, and a life event sets the blaze. Thankfully, you're not helpless in mitigating some of the factors. You can't predict where lightning will strike or when a meth lab will explode. But you can water and you can clear.

Be a well-watered man. Callus your hands piling the slash. And when fires break out, lead by lovingly initiating conversations that extinguish each blaze at the source. Steward your communication acreage well and watch your marital forest flourish under your care.

> **KEY TAKEAWAY**
> Bridle your tongue. Be well-watered.
> Steward your acreage to the glory of God.

MEDIOCRITY VS MASTERY

Mediocrity	*Mastery*
Fiery, unbridled tongue	Bridled tongue; speaks with caution and care
Unwatered by the Word; undisciplined spiritually	Well-watered; washes wife with the water of the Word (Ephesians 5:26)
Lets marital tinder accumulate	Diligently pursues conversations that clear out relational tinder
Stands idle through tough events; fails to engage and lead	Responds quickly and decisively to unforeseen events; leads wife through

APPLICATION QUESTIONS

Taking the passages from James to heart, what are two ways you can bridle your tongue?

What are common sources of tinder buildup in your marriage? What causes frustration between you and typically goes unresolved? Can you think of anything right now?

As a husband, what "cleanup conversation" feels most pressing? How can you initiate that talk with your bride today?

CHAPTER NINE

THE WARTIME AND THE PEACETIME

Responding to the Seasonal Sways of Married Life

> *Blessed are the peacemakers,*
> *for they will be called children of God.*
> Matthew 5:9 NIV

Every married couple swings between communication peacetimes and wartimes. Each season is inevitable, but what's not inevitable is that you will handle them well. Thankfully, there are strategies couples can use during communication peacetimes *and* wartimes that will strengthen their marriage and build skills for quick recoveries if and when wartime breaks out.

THE SCARCITY SWITCH

After Selena's grandma passed away, we were sorting through some of her belongings and found ourselves marveling at what she had kept. We wondered why on earth Vera had kept *so* many cans and boxes of food even though they had expired a decade before. She held onto furniture that had seen (much) better days, trinkets you'd find at a flea market in the three-dollars-or-less bin, and boxes of old magazines filled with stories that had long since faded from relevance.

We were genuinely puzzled; Vera wasn't a hoarder by any stretch of the word. *Why in the world did she keep all this stuff?* Then we had an elucidating conversation with Selena's mom.

"It's because she grew up after the Depression," she told us.

We gathered that grandma had lived through wars and scarcity like we've never experienced. For her, this was a way of gaining an iota of certainty in a time of great instability. Vera's collecting habits started to make sense. Managing scarcity had become a way of life. It was the lens through which she viewed the world. And if you've adulted through the early 2020s, you can sympathize a bit.

As I write this, just a few years ago people lost their ever-loving minds thinking they might run out of toilet paper. A friend told me that he was walking through his neighborhood and saw a woman closing the door on her garage, which was filled to the brim with Costco-sized packages of 4-ply quilted white gold. You'd think a clean derrière was a matter of life and death! For some, perhaps.

Selena and I managed not to get caught up in the TP hysteria, but we did make sure we had plenty of food stored up. A switch gets flipped in our minds when faced with adversity, and it's an entirely different mentality. During peacetime, you're freed from thinking about survival and you can focus on higher-order concerns like passion, desire, and recreation (to name a few). Then, when wartime hits, you measure what matters more carefully. In that mindset, you'll go to great lengths to prepare to weather the storm well.

Couples are bound to endure swings between peacetime and wartime. The question is, how will you use the peacetime to build systems that sustain you through war, and when wartime does hit, how will you navigate the storm and get to the other side better than before?

In the coming chapters you will build awareness, tools, and skills to communicate better in your marriage. Some will apply in wartime, others will apply in peacetime. Many of them you will find useful for both. Before you can start filling your marital war chest and preparing your peacetime plans, you need to be able to accurately identify what communication dispensation you're in.

PEACETIME AND WARTIME DEFINED

Marital peacetime means experiencing *consistent closeness and clear communication*. Typically, peacetime means you're having quality conversations, building a mutually satisfying intimate life, laughing, and tackling weighty issues with unity. During marital peacetimes, all is well in house and home. With your nuptial borders secure, you're freed to focus on work, ministry, projects, and fun.

Wartime is the complete opposite. Whether wartime manifests through long-term marital neglect, or it's kicked off through some inciting event, it's a miserable place to be. During marital wartime, you're chronically disconnected, you can't manage a conversation of any substance without it degrading into a fight or one of you vacating the room. You drift steadily toward isolation and your intimate life suffers. Your friendship is iced and neither of you shows signs of thawing. You can't focus at work because you're replaying last night's argument in your head and tallying up the score. You feel tempted to seek comfort in old vices—pornography, substance abuse, or screen-binging in your infinity app of choice. You want to fight the urges, but you're in survival mode. You need relief.

Nay, what you actually need is *peace*.

HEAD HARBINGERS OF PEACE

Peace happens because peacemakers make it. It's true in the *domus* and it's true on the globe. As the Christ proxy in the marriage, the husband is the primary peacemaker in the home. Wives are peacemakers, too, and sustained peace requires mutuality, but husbands lead the charge as they mimic Christ, our supreme and reigning harbinger of peace.

As Jesus taught in the Sermon on the Mount, "Blessed are the peacemakers, for they will be called children of God" (Matthew 5:9 NIV). To which James added, "a harvest of righteousness is sown in peace by those who make peace" (James 3:18). Husband, you are commissioned into the business of making peace with an end in mind. Those who make peace not only attain it, but they are declared blessed children of God who reap a harvest of righteousness. What God-fearing man wouldn't want to make peace? No man I know. But, as it happens, there's work in the making.

Since the term *peacemaker* (εἰρηνοποιός) only occurs once in the New Testament, its lexical definition is markedly simple. This makes application a breeze, though the work, not so much.

Peacemaking means "to *endeavor* to reconcile persons who have disagreements."⁶ Ah, there it is. The work.

Peacemaking means you must *endeavor* to reconcile. If a husband hopes to substantiate peace in his home, he is commanded to aim, struggle, venture, exert, strive, grind, determine, take pains, or, as the idiom goes, give it the ol' college try. And, if at first you don't succeed, college try it again. Or something.

Men who make peace must endeavor to do so. Peace doesn't make itself. So take whatever synonym for *endeavor* that resonates most with you, and run with it. But before you do, let's explore some practical strategies.

"THE BEST-LAID PLANS OF MICE AND MEN OFT GO ASTRAY"

Peacemaking is as much a peacetime activity as it is a wartime charge. And a winning wartime strategy requires a doubly winning peacetime plan. It's *during* the peacetime that you establish your wartime protocols. It's the time when you build up your defenses, establish rules of engagement, and create backup plans for how to de-escalate tensions before the nukes breach the brims of their silos. Some actions are proactive and preventative, while others are of the break-glass-in-case-of-emergency persuasion. Either now or in your next peacetime, endeavor these four things.

1. Establish your baseline.

Discuss and agree upon the concepts of peacetime and wartime communication. Are you clear on how each season looks in your relationship? What does each typically entail? How has wartime erupted in the past? What patterns of timing, mood,

---

6. Frederick W. Danker, ed., *A Greek-English Lexicon of the New Testament and Other Early Christian Literature*, 3rd ed. (Chicago: University of Chicago Press, 2000), 288.

blood sugar, tone, and surrounding events begin to emerge? Talk about it. Flip on the lights and swing wide every door of your relationship to make sure all is visible and understood.

2. Write your wartime accords.

What qualifies as acceptable and unacceptable communication during conflict? You need to discuss, agree on, and write down a plan. Then, if desired, sign it. It need not be a lengthy plan, but it should be clear. We'll cover this in more detail in chapter 11, "The Brothel and the Barn."

3. Build peacetime routines.

Peace is made and remade through built-in rhythms of life. Don't be surprised when you're drifting apart while neither of you is paddling. Design routines to keep you connected by default. Morning coffee, evening wine, scheduled intimacy (not lame at all, I promise). You need time and space to be married and to do as marrieds do. Work, kids, and life are insatiable creatures eager to devour all in their path. Everything encroaches. Endeavor to establish sacred, sovereign peacekeeping space for just you and your wife. Then defend your borders.

4. Plan for de-escalation.

Finally, what will you do when diplomatic relations sour? You alone know what Threat Level Midnight looks like for your marriage. Talk about how you will proactively de-escalate tensions when you sense war breaking out. What will you say? As the husband, how will you initiate the peacemaking endeavor? Does your wife know how she will respond to your leadership? Will you have a "pause clause" or something like it that allows one or both of you to temporarily tap out? As we've found, making time and space to process in a healthy manner is vital to healthy reconciliation. Use this time to cool off, seek counsel from trusted friends, and get emotional or physical rest (though I don't recommend spending the night away from your bed). Then, what's your timeframe for returning to the conversation in order to reconcile? Establish these protocols ahead of time, so when things get murky, you have a clear plan.

Whatever your plan, remember to execute when it matters. Don't just pack the chute, pull the ripcord. Just not too late.

> **KEY TAKEAWAY**
> Peacemaking is as much a peacetime activity as it is a wartime charge. Both need a plan.

MEDIOCRITY VS MASTERY

Mediocrity	Mastery
Unable to see or de-escalate rising tensions	Owns his role as the chief peacemaker in the home
Passive; allows prolonged wartime (even cold war)	Leads his wife and household in making peacetime routines
Refuses to make peacetime and wartime strategies	Initiates in executing wartime strategies; does so lovingly and gently

APPLICATION QUESTIONS

What does peacetime look like for your marriage? Write down a few key aspects of your communication that are typical of the peacetimes you experience. Jot down 2–3 new ideas for "peacekeeping spaces" you can share with your wife.

Think of the last season of "wartime" you had with your wife. What was it about? How did it escalate?

Given the last question, what could you have done to endeavor more diligently to make peace in your home? Give specific examples.

CHAPTER TEN

THE PRECISION AND THE POWER
Defining and Defeating the Husband Paradox

> *Likewise, husbands, live with your wives in an understanding way, showing honor to the woman as the weaker vessel, since they are heirs with you of the grace of life, so that your prayers may not be hindered.*
> 1 Peter 3:7

Be tough *for* your wife, but always tender *with* her. Those are words I wish I would've heard as a young husband. So many early communication missteps could have been avoided.

I, like many husbands (especially young ones), conflated logic with love and too often pitted facts against feelings. I was an expert at being correct, and oh boy, did Selena know it! Being correct only equates to being right *some* of the time.

TITANS OF INDUSTRY

Heavy machinery mesmerizes me. It's the perfect picture of power and precision. So much so that the algorithmic overlords on social media exploit my interest. To keep me scrolling, my feeds have morphed to include a steady drip of bulldozers, metallurgical factories, forestry equipment, and the like. Also memes from *The Office*, but that's a separate thing.

What astounds me most about heavy machinery—namely, hydraulic earthmoving equipment—is how powerful *and* precise they can be. In the hands of a skilled operator, the same excavator that plucks a two-ton stump from the ground can be used to snuff a candle at the wick. I once saw a guy cut a cucumber in half with a knife taped to the claw of his seventy-two-inch excavator bucket. And the cucumber was balancing on a balloon, which didn't pop.

These gentle giants are the same machines that weigh fifty tons and move literal mountains. They're machines that do *work*. Real, difficult, important, work.

Like you.

HEADSHIP, WORK, AND WORDS

You were made to work. Even in Eden, Adam worked. Some mistakenly think that a sinless planet would've been nothing but navel gazing and grape grazing. Not even close. After creating mankind, God said, "Be fruitful and multiply and fill the earth and subdue it, and have dominion over [it]" (Genesis 1:28). In other words, do work. And do it unto God's glory, because he made it and called it good. It's *toil* that gives good work a bad name. Toil came with the fall, along with labor pains, thorns, and yappy dogs.

This cultural mandate—to have dominion over creation through work and fruitfulness—was given to men and women alike, but their expressions are unique. As much as some try to erase differences between the sexes, they exist. And saying so is an act of modern rebellion. But Christian rebellion doesn't stop with proclaiming truth. We must dare to live it.

Biblically speaking, men were assigned and designed to be heads, and women were assigned and designed to be helpers. These differences do not equal disparities in worth or importance, but in role. Why is this relevant? Along with each head and helper assignment comes, generally speaking, specialized inclinations and responsibilities. For example, why are most coal miners men and nurses tend to be women? They are *inclined* to be. Populations naturally sort toward biologically delineated inclinations regardless of income disparity. The data bears this out even and *especially* in staunchly egalitarian societies like Denmark and Norway.[7]

Men are stronger and women more nurturing. Men are prone to toughness and women are prone to tenderness. And, similar to how toil is a distortion of good work, there are distortions in inclination, which bring toil into how men communicate with their wives.

THE HUSBAND'S PARADOX

Toil-free toughness is the godly man's goal. It's the kind you employ to finish a hard task, to make good on your promises, to solve impossible problems, and to lift heavy things without throwing out your back. But beware, there's also a *toilish* toughness that will wreak havoc in your life like a coyote in a bunny hutch.

This is where the husband's paradox comes in. As the man, you are inclined to think, work, and act as a man put to work in the task God assigned. Ideally, you do this in your job, at church, with your family, and in your marriage. But you do each

---

7. Erik Mac Giolla and Petri J. Kajonius, "Sex Differences in Personality are Larger in Gender Equal Countries: Replicating and Extending a Surprising Finding," International Journal of Psychology 54, no. 6 (September 11, 2018): 705–711, https://doi.org/10.1002/ijop.12529.

job *differently* as each context requires. If not, chaos ensues. For example, if you instruct your kids like you train your coworkers or if you talk to your pastor like you talk to your wife, something's wrong. Or, for the purposes of this book, if you talk to your wife like she's one of the guys or treat her like a mere coworker, Peter and Paul would like to have a word with you.

Peter wrote, "Likewise, husbands, live with your wives in an understanding way, showing honor to the woman as the weaker vessel, since they are heirs with you of the grace of life, so that your prayers may not be hindered" (1 Peter 3:7). As moderns, we're tempted to read a pejorative sense into the idea of wives being the "weaker vessel," but Peter isn't dunking on women. He's making an observation.

He's only saying that since husbands are generally physically stronger, larger, and more imposing, they must be *watchful* to not misuse their strength at home, lest they distort their role as head, misrepresent Christ, and mishandle their wives. A man is never to use his strength to his advantage in marriage. To do so is an affront to your wife, rebellion from God, and an insult to headship. Don't be surprised when your prayers are hindered while you mishandle your bride.

In the same vein, Paul added, "Husbands, love your wives, and do not be harsh with them" (Colossians 3:19). In other words, be gentle with her. She is not a man, she is not tough like you (though she is undoubtedly tough in ways you aren't), and she was never meant to contend with you. She was meant to be loved by you, cherished, gently stewarded as the gift she is.

Be tough *for* your wife but always tender *with* her. Succeed in both and you have debunked the husband paradox.

PRACTICAL GENTLENESS

In case you're wondering, here are three specific examples of gentleness in communication.

Listening charitably

"Love hopes all things." Expect the best while your wife speaks. Lower your defenses, hear her heart, and remember she loves you. Then respond in love.

Manner matters

Carry yourself with gentleness toward your bride, especially in how you speak to her. Do not be harsh in word, manner, tone, or facial expression.

Overlooking offenses and annoyances

During pregnancy, Selena lost the ability to name nouns. "Can you get that thing over there?" was a question that drove me nuts. *I'm not a mind reader, woman!* Still, it was a chance to ask gently for her to clarify instead of firing back some annoyed retort. Whatever your wife does that annoys (or angers) you, it's always possible to respond gently.

HAND TO THE PLOW

Like a heavy machine, you were made to do good, difficult, and meaningful work. It's hardwired into your DNA, and I pray you do so unto God's glory. Make your hands rough with work as you gladly labor with vigor and mastery for the good of the order.

But be ever watchful that the toughness your work requires faces outward from your doorstep while your tenderness faces inward. It's not a paradox to be gentle and strong at the same time. King Christ is both the Lion of Judah and the Lamb who was slain. Fight for your wife like a lion, die for her like a lamb.

> **KEY TAKEAWAY**
> Toil-free toughness blended with gentleness is the godly man's goal.

MEDIOCRITY VS MASTERY

Mediocrity	*Mastery*
Makes no distinction between work talk and husband-to-wife communication	Keeps toughness pointed outward
Treats wife like one of the guys	Deals more gently with his wife than with others
Deals harshly through word choice, tone, or manner	Especially careful with word choice, tone, and manner at home

APPLICATION QUESTIONS

Consider your outward-facing roles and relationships. What is different about how you treat your friends and coworkers versus how you speak with your wife?

Fill in the table on the next page. Try to think of two to three specific descriptors for each space.

	When Speaking with Friends and Colleagues	When Speaking with Your Wife	When Speaking with Your Children (Extra Credit)
Word Choice			
Tone			
Manner			

CHAPTER ELEVEN

THE BROTHEL AND THE BARN
Wielding Your Words to Build What is Good

Death and life are in the power of the tongue, and those who love it will eat its fruits.
Proverbs 18:21

Many things are best left unsaid, particularly in marriage. Early in our marriage, by God's grace, Selena and I resolved that we'd never say *divorce*. We promised to never use it as a threat, as a passing mention during a difficult season, or as a grumbled suggestion under our breath in a moment of emotional exasperation. That rule remains today, and in hindsight, it has set the trajectory of many of our fiercest disagreements and seen us through to the other side.

BROTHEL OR BARN?

Words have power because they carry meaning. This chapter's verse, a proverb, confirms it most precisely. "Death and life are in the power of the tongue." Does the tongue literally kill? If, in the mouth of a despot, his tongue orders killing, perhaps. Still, the tongue only uttered the words. It's the words that carry the meaning, and the meaning conveys the tyrant's intention to kill. The tongue is a tool, and like any tool, it can be used to build or to destroy. As Doug Wilson says, "Hammers are used to build both brothels and barns."[8]

Banning the word *divorce* from our vocab was the start of barn-building in our marriage. It provided for us the occasion to set our communication ground rules, which I'll discuss below, but first I want to ask, what is the point of banned language in marriage? To ask another way, should marriage be a free-speech zone? I don't think so.

Before you're too triggered by the idea of banned speech, rest assured, I've read Orwell and Huxley too. I'm not suggesting you establish a mini Ministry of Truth within your covenant. Unlike Big Brother's intention in *1984,* prohibited language in marriage is not a matter of control, but of wisdom. And it's wise to never say some things.

Your words are your hammer. Are you building a brothel or a barn?

Are you building a place for your family to flourish? Or a deathly alternative?

COMMUNICATION GROUND RULES

Jesus echoes Solomon's point, but stronger, "I tell you, on the day of judgment people will give account for every careless word they speak, for by your words you will be justified, and

---

8. Doug Wilson, *Ploductivity* (Moscow, ID: Canon Press, 2020), 29.

by your words you will be condemned" (Matthew 12:36–37). He who has ears, let him hear! In context, Jesus is talking to the Pharisees about the fruit they bear. He draws a clarion connection between the words they say and the heart from whence the words flow. It's biblical through and through. Your heart is the fount of everything you say.

Your words carry immense weight and responsibility in your wife's heart. Not only your words, but the culture of words you endorse in the home. As a gatekeeper for your household, will you allow speech that tears down, or will you champion that which builds up? You need a filter, or a *standard*, that governs acceptable speech in your marriage. Except, instead of an Orwellian Ministry of Truth which dictates and censors with no consideration for heart, you need God's Word and a good set of communication ground rules.

OFF-LIMITS, UNHELPFUL, AND WISE

With marriage being the partnership that it is, creating good communication ground rules is a task to tag-team. As you and your wife think through how your family's word culture should look, the three categories below should prove helpful.

Category 1: Off-Limits

This category includes any words, phrases, or manners of speech that can *only* hurt your wife or marriage. These are the things you know you should never say but still might say in a heated moment. It seems obvious, but I'm still amazed at how some couples speak to one another.

"I should have never married you!"

"You're nothing but a (insert degrading phrase)."

"You're such a (expletive name)."

"I hate you."

Again, these types of phrases and words are obviously hurtful, but they need to be outlined and explicitly excised from your marriage before tensions rise. That way in a heated moment you both know the rules of engagement. (Using self-control to not say them is a different discussion.)

Universally speaking, the word *divorce*, name-calling, degrading speech, and language the Bible calls "reviling" all tidily fall into the things-never-to-be-said category. Be sure to outlaw hateful, hurtful language intended to harm, kill, and destroy. What life can this type of communication possibly bring? None at all, so put it to death.

Category 2: Unhelpful

This will be the grayest area of your communication ground rules. It includes things that are imprecise or lazy. For Selena and me, unhelpful phrases that aren't inherently unhealthy include the use of absolutes. This could also include exaggeration and hyperbole.

Here are a few examples:

"You're always late."

"You never want sex."

"You're always critical."

"You ruin everything!"

You can get a sense of the sentiment beneath each phrase, and there may even be a scrap of truth behind each one. Still, the phrases themselves undermine useful communication; they're just not helpful. They don't get anywhere. They're the verbal equivalent of peeling out on wet pavement. There's noise and slight movement, but you're going nowhere. Here's one absolute statement: always avoid absolutes.

Sarcasm is also unhelpful. It's the cheapest form of humor because it buys laughs at someone else's expense. Couples who are fluent in sarcasm will struggle to feel safe in their communication since serious conversations rarely materialize and are often derailed if they do.

Take time to do the work of finding more precise language to express what you mean. Identify habits, ruts, words, and common modes of communicating that are unhelpful for building up your wife and your marriage, then spend your communication efforts practicing wisdom instead.

Category 3: Wise

This third category is where the tongue has the power of life Solomon described. Categorically wise language includes honest encouragement (not flattery), affection, endearment, gratitude, questions rooted in genuine interest, good-natured humor, and any exhortation in God's Word, to name a few. Wise words build up, make stronger, heal, endear, and more than anything, they glorify God.

BLUEPRINTS FOR BARN BUILDERS

Let's say your marriage is an empty plot of land, you're homesteaders, and your words are your hammer. What are you going to build? A brothel or a barn?

How you answer depends on which blueprints you're holding. A good set of communication ground rules is the blueprint for couples building big, beautiful, event-venue-worthy barns with their words. Make the time to write yours, have the conversations, and as the husband, determine today that your house is one that uses words wisely to build and never to destroy.

> **KEY TAKEAWAY**
> Your words carry immense weight and responsibility in your wife's heart. Choose them wisely.

MEDIOCRITY VS MASTERY

Mediocrity	*Mastery*
Uses words haphazardly based on emotions, habit, or ease	Chooses words with surgical precision, especially when emotions are a factor
Draws no clear boundaries to govern marital diction	Takes care to establish communication ground rules
Fails to adhere to pre-established communication boundaries when tensions rise	Wisely refuses to breach boundaries

APPLICATION QUESTIONS

How would you characterize the communication culture in your household? Write down three to five phrases or words that describe it.

How would your wife describe your communication culture? Ask her and jot a few notes below.

Do you have communication ground rules? Why or why not? If not, what steps can you take today to get them started?

CHAPTER TWELVE

THE LOVER AND THE BELOVED
The Blessing of Communication Before, During, and After Sex

> *My beloved speaks and says to me:*
> *"Arise, my love, my beautiful one,*
> *and come away,*
> *for behold, the winter is past;*
> *the rain is over and gone."*
> Song of Solomon 2:10–11

Much of this book deals with occasions for communication and tools to handle them as opposed to specific topics. This is because the content of communication varies widely from couple to couple. Instead of prescribing what to say, I've presented tools to help you think through *how* you say it. While I can't rip your boards for you, I can point you to the table saw. *Teach a man to fish...* and all.

With that said, there is one particular topic most couples face with varying degrees of agony, so I thought it worthy of its own chapter. That topic is sex.

Acts of intimacy and the discussions surrounding it are rightly vulnerable and prone to sensitivity. This means conversations about your expectations, hopes, desires, and even frustrations with your sex life can be difficult to have. Still, that's not my angle with this chapter. I trust the other tools in this book will help you have productive conversations *about* your sex life since I'd say it falls under the "difficult conversations" category, which is addressed elsewhere.

Here, I'd like to talk about how you communicate in an *intimate manner toward one another* before, during, and even after sex. Specifically, what sorts of sexual phrases, words, allusions, and the like are appropriate and godly for Christian men speaking to their Christian wives? What should he anticipate and aim for as he seeks to "arouse love" in and from his bride?

Much to a lover's delight, even these questions have answers in Scripture. And hearty ones at that.

THE SONG OF ALL SONGS

The Song of Songs is a masterclass on intimate communication, and its canonicity tells us something too. Just the mere fact that the Song is part of the Bible demonstrates the weight of its content. The question of how to speak throughout intimacy is an important one, and talk between lovers, while private, is good to get right. Sensual speech toward one's spouse is speech blessed by God. And, not only does intimacy matter, but how we *communicate intimately* matters as well.

The title, Song of Songs, also emphasizes the book's place among poetic literature. It is the song of all songs, superlative, masterful, elevated, supreme. As one commentator notes, the title could be construed as it is "the very best" of all songs.[9] The Song of Songs is not just a flyover book in the Bible! It's a masterpiece worthy of appreciation and application alike. Sorry, songwriters—eat your hearts out. Despite their tenacity, Tenacious D didn't actually write the greatest song in the world, Solomon did.

SENSUALLY SPEAKING

Though interpretation (and thus, application) of the Song varies widely among scholars, most agree that it's clearly sensual poetry expressing romantic love between a young man and a young woman in marriage. Though much of the imagery is foreign to our modern minds, make no mistake, the book is unquestionably steamy.

Given that, let's look at four themes from the Song of Solomon that show us how spouses might communicate sensually in marriage. Also, note that my use of the word *erotic* shouldn't indicate carnality or lust in sensual communication but rather the overtly sexual nature of the themes observed.

1. *Erotic Physical Admiration*

The Song is littered with examples of the lover and the beloved complimenting one another's physical appearance. It's not just that they're attractive folks in an objective sense, it's that they're especially charmed *by each other.*

Of the woman, the young man says, "Behold, you are beautiful, my love, behold, you are beautiful!" (Song 4:1). He goes on to systematically admire her many features. Her eyes,

---

9. Commentary on Song of Solomon 1:1 from The ESV Study Bible (Wheaton, IL: Crossway, 2008), 1216.

hair, neck, lips, and even her breasts are mentioned. Every facet of her body is delightful to him. Finally, as if to throw his hands up in resignation at her perfection, he concludes, "You are altogether beautiful, my love; there is no flaw in you" (Song 4:7). She is flawless in his eyes, and he *must* tell her so. Then, the young woman reciprocates.

Of him, she says, "My beloved is radiant and ruddy, distinguished among ten thousand" (Song 5:10). Then, just as he did, she goes on to systematically admire his features, from his head down to his column-like legs (since apparently he never skipped leg day) and back up to his mouth. There is no doubt that this woman thinks her husband is a physical specimen to behold. And there is no doubt that she wants him to know it. So she tells him overtly.

As readers we should note that these statements are not mere observations, they're erotic admirations *with an end goal in mind*. They're expressing a deep desire to see their emotional love physically consummated in the act of making love. They're anticipating intimacy, which is the next theme we'll explore.

2. *Erotic Anticipation*

In the Song both the lover and the beloved desperately crave one another. Their expressions of admiration carry with them full *anticipation* of their sexual appetites being satiated. They're not content admiring the ocean from the observation deck. They want to wade deep in its waters and be awash in its waves.

The woman says, "I adjure you, O daughters of Jerusalem, if you find my beloved, that you tell him I am *sick with love*" (Song 5:8, emphasis added). Also, "Let my beloved come to his garden, and eat its choicest fruits" (Song 4:16). Her love is invitational and she's not content with mere observation. She calls herself *his* garden, not just to be admired but to be tasted and consumed. Like I said, things get steamy.

Of course, the man is not silent and his language is equally rousing. He says things like, "Your navel is a rounded bowl that never lacks mixed wine. Your belly is a heap of wheat," (Song 7:2) and "Your stature is like a palm tree, and your breasts are like its clusters. I say I will *climb* the palm tree and *lay hold of its fruit*. Oh may your breasts be like clusters of the vine, and the scent of your breath like apples" (Song 7:7–8, emphasis added).

His terminology may seem odd to us—to the point of inciting belly laughs from countless schoolboys past—but it's clear that this is *not* passive language. It's language of partaking, enjoying, and experiencing. After all, what does a man do with bowls of mixed wine, heaps of wheat, and clusters of fruit? He drinks deep, his appetite is satisfied, and he delights in their flavor.

3. Mutual Conversation

The Song of Solomon is not a monologue. Both the lover and the beloved contribute to the conversation, mutually giving of and receiving their words and themselves. As the young woman says in multiple places, "I am my beloved's and my beloved is mine" (Song 6:3). They've both given themselves over to each other, which is evident even in the *manner* of their back-and-forth exchange.

The takeaway here is that sensual communication is a dance and both partners must participate for it to work. In practical application, one spouse may initiate the communication, but it takes two to verbally tango. Otherwise, things can get weird fast. The solution? Have a discussion (or many) about how sensual communication might function in your relationship. When does it work? When does it decidedly *not* work? What are your expectations? What sorts of language will you use? And what makes you both feel most comfortable *and* aroused? To help with this, let's look at the next theme.

4. Edifying Talk

When it comes to bedroom talk, there's a line that can be crossed, and it's not always clear where it lies. While the language of Song of Solomon is intensely sensual, it's also decent. The warning here is to avoid language which might cheapen sex or degrade one another, as such speech dishonors your spouse, pollutes the marriage bed, and dishonors God.

"Marriage is to be held in honor among all, and the marriage bed is to be undefiled" (Hebrews 13:4 NASB). While the author of Hebrews was referring to things like fornication and adultery, I would argue that the words uttered in the bedroom must be carefully curated so as to not import defiling practices and fantasies from unholy sources (think R-rated movies, porn, explicit books and music). In other words, speak to your wife with the honor and admiration that befits her. And speak of sex as the treasure God created it to be. Keep it classy. Your words need not be lewd to have the desired effect.

YOUR TURN

In an ideal marriage, both husband and wife are committed to giving their whole selves over to each other for their whole lives. It's to that end that you're reading this book. You probably want to learn to communicate well with your wife so you might love her better.

Similarly, learning to speak sensually is an opportunity to love your wife (and her, you) in new and profound ways. The Song of

Solomon has shown us just how spirited sensual talk can get. I'll leave it up to you and your beloved to take it from here.

> **KEY TAKEAWAY**
> The question of how to speak throughout intimacy is an important one, and talk between lovers, while private, is good to get right. Sensual speech toward one's spouse is speech blessed by God.

MEDIOCRITY VS MASTERY

Mediocrity	Mastery
Doesn't value communication during intimacy	Understands the importance of communication throughout intimacy
Avoids talking about sensual speech	Seeks to have candid conversations about what works and doesn't work
Uses sensual speech to self-satisfy	Uses sensual speech to edify his wife

APPLICATION QUESTIONS

Would you say you and your wife feel comfortable speaking sensually to one another before, during, and after sex? Why or why not?

How might being thoughtful about sensual speech improve your intimate life?

As a challenge, I encourage you to set aside an evening in the near future to talk to your wife specifically about this topic. How can you start that conversation? Jot down a brief outline of what you might say.

CHAPTER THIRTEEN

THE CLARITY AND THE PEN
The Utility of Writing to Say All You Mean

Whoever restrains his words has knowledge, and he who has a cool spirit is a man of understanding.
Proverbs 17:27

Clear communication requires clear thinking, and one key to thinking clearly is to write.

Take this book, for example. The sentences you're reading are the result of many rounds of planning, outlining, writing, rewriting, editing, and proofing. By the time your eyes land on these words they will be the best version of themselves they can be, barring editorial flubs. And I'll tell you, books have a way of transforming into unexpected creatures by the time they hit the presses.

You wouldn't believe the number of missteps, half-baked ideas, and poorly worded sentences that have been captured, slayed, and discarded along the way. That is the wonder of writing. It forces an author to communicate with a clarity and depth not always present in the spoken word. And this is especially true in marriage. In this chapter, I'll make the case that writing letters to your wife is a vital skill that will greatly improve the quality of your communication with her.

SQUEEZERS GET WHAT SQUEEZERS DESERVE

Words are a force to be restrained like a rottweiler on a leash. Solomon wrote, "Whoever restrains his words has knowledge" (Proverbs 17:27). His meaning is clear, but consider how one might restrain words. Once something is said, how can you take it back? You can't. You can explain, seek forgiveness, or ask for mental redaction, but once you've tolled the verbal bell, it can't be unrung. It's like that time when my dad, in a moment of intense sincerity, cussed out loud while leading prayer for a large group of people. Good luck getting that toothpaste back in the tube. If you don't want Aquafresh all over the counter, you'll do best not to squeeze.

Solomon was advising against squeezing. Word restraint happens before you speak, in the mind. It happens with understanding, or the ability to anticipate the effects of words without having to try them on for size. In another passage he wrote, "When there are many words, wrongdoing is unavoidable, but one who restrains his lips is wise" (Proverbs 10:19 NASB). There is a form of verbal processing that leads to sin. And verbal vomit never makes anyone well.

Are you wise? Are you a man of understanding? Your ability to restrain words and speak clearly will tell. But even men of understanding veer off the verbal rails from time to time. As familiarity grows, decorum and clarity don't always follow. This is true particularly when you're married. Also, when you're tired, emotionally down, in conflict, or if you're not exactly sure what to say. This is why writing to speak is a must-have tool for marital communication mastery.

TO THE PEN!

The pen is the ultimate communication clarifier. Here are some specific upsides of writing as a means of articulating what you mean more clearly.

Editability

Writing forces you to think before every word. Unlike spoken missteps, penned mistakes can be undone. And redone. And redone again. This is the fifth time I've written this sentence. That's the beauty of writing—you'll never know how terrible the first four drafts were. The pen affords you an opportunity for extraordinary clarity with your wife.

Lexical Novelty

Mix up your word choice. To this end, a good thesaurus is a veritable treasure trove for weary word weavers. Take time to change things up. When it comes to writing, you don't have to do what you always do. As long as you're honest and not too cheesy, you can find new ways to express what you want to say. You'll often say more than you meant along the way—but in a good way.

Language is a smorgasbord of words, idioms, sounds, and expressions. Explore the breadth of the buffet. Skip the cold pizza and try the gravlax. You might hate it. Or you might not.

Deliberateness

Writing forces you to think carefully and attentively about *what* you want to say.

Have you ever gone a few days with something bothering you? I have and I do. And until I stop and ask, *What is actually troubling me?* I'll just continue on despite being perturbed. Perhaps you can relate. Putting words to what I'm feeling is not something that comes naturally.

Broadly speaking, women are better at expressing their emotions. Men must work at it. While exceptions to both generalizations exist, the point is that by writing a letter to your wife, you are slowing down enough to plumb your own heart, thoughts, and emotions to find words that express exactly what you need to say. We don't often have that chance during conversation. With writing, you do.

Disarmament

Is there something you haven't said to your wife because you're afraid of how she'll respond? Writing can help. Handwritten letters have a way of disarming defenses and allowing your wife to respond with the same thoughtfulness with which you wrote. She'll have her reaction either way—reasonably, she needs time to process and respond to whatever issue you've raised—but this way you'll have said all that needs to be said in the most thoughtful manner you can muster. Consider exchanging multiple letters with your wife if needed as you work through a tough subject. The conversation may not be easier, but it might be healthier. It's harder to argue or interrupt when paper is the medium.

If you haven't brought something up because you're ashamed, it's too painful, or because you're not sure how your wife will respond, take to the pen. The conversation *needs* to happen, and fast. A handwritten letter may be the best next step.

Tough talks are still tough on paper, but *less*.

The Letter Effect

Finally, who doesn't enjoy reading a handwritten letter? There's nothing like it because there's no way to fake it. They can't be copied and pasted or mass produced. Direct mail marketers have tried, but you can always tell. A handwritten letter is like good Scotch. By virtue of what it is, you know whoever made it took their time and not a single corner was cut.

I'm not a betting man, but I'd bet paper money that your wife would love a handwritten letter from you. Even more importantly, she'll feel loved by you. Isn't that the point of communication anyway?

THE MEDIUM AND THE MESSAGE

Sometimes all you need to clarify your marital communication is a change of venue and pace. The handwritten word offers both. For the masterful communicator, writing to speak is an indispensable tool to learn.

Go for it. Try your hand at the pen. You need not be Shakespeare, Hemingway, or Sorkin. Just be you, but on paper. What you write may surprise the both of you.

> **KEY TAKEAWAY**
> Writing to your wife is an invaluable tool for fresh, thoughtful communication, particularly when it concerns difficult topics.

MEDIOCRITY VS MASTERY

Mediocrity	*Mastery*
Rarely restrains his words; shoots harmfully from the hip	Skilled word restrainer; speaks with caution
Overly content with well-worn words and phrases	Interested in discovering new ways to articulate his affection
Sees writing as impossible or too difficult to try	Willing to write when extraordinary clarity is needed

APPLICATION QUESTIONS

Think of a time when you've said something you wished you didn't. How could you have thought or acted differently to restrain your words?

In general, do you consider yourself a clear communicator? Why or why not?

How might writing help you clarify and help your communication with your wife?

Challenge: Write your wife a letter. I'll let you choose the topic. You can even mail it to her (at your own address) for added effect. As a bonus, ask her to write you back.

CHAPTER FOURTEEN

THE ROAD AND THE RANGER
How Tough Talks Bring About Unexpected Blessing

> *This is the message we have heard from him and proclaim to you, that God is light, and in him is no darkness at all. If we say we have fellowship with him while we walk in darkness, we lie and do not practice the truth. But if we walk in the light, as he is in the light, we have fellowship with one another, and the blood of Jesus his Son cleanses us from all sin.*
> 1 John 1:5–7

If at all possible, never refuse a road trip. It's a rule to live by. Because, when you say yes to a road trip, you say yes to adventure. At least that's my experience.

It was certainly the case when my friend John asked me if I wanted to drive with him from the Pacific Northwest to Savannah, Georgia. John had just gotten out of the army, and he needed to get his truck and belongings back home. On a whim, he asked if I wanted to go, and before he could finish I interrupted, "Absolutely I will!" We were set to leave within a few days.

Now, half the fun of going on a road trip is the planning, and since John was in the throes of exiting the army, he let me choose the route. When you traverse the United States from Washington to Georgia, you basically have two choices: low or high. If you take the southern route, you get to see the Grand Canyon, Arches, and Zion (and other orange rocks). Or you can take the northern route and go through Montana, the Badlands, and Mount Rushmore. I had already seen most of the southwest, and since we both really wanted to see a bunch of presidential faces carved into a mountain, I chose the high road, and we were off.

We made great time. After the first day we were within striking distance of our primary target: Mount Rushmore. Our anticipation was building, but the only problem was the timing. We ended up hitting the monument after dark. We both saw this coming, but based on the postcards we had seen with the rock faces lit up at night, we assumed there would be lights. After all, you can't shut down an entire mountain, can you?

Well, apparently you can. And they do.

When we arrived, the park was empty and the gates locked tight.

"Ah, man!" John protested. "It's the whole reason we took this route!"

"No way!" I was flabbergasted.

We commiserated for a moment, then an opportunity presented itself. Only the park *entrance* was locked. The exit gate was wide open! Without hesitation, John sped up the exit, but not before I saw a pair of headlights flash from around the corner. I thought nothing of it.

We reached the top of the parking structure, and it was windy and dark, so we dug around in the truck bed for our coats. We figured even with the monument lights off we'd be able to see *something*.

Within seconds I saw the same pair of headlights pull up behind us. Sure enough, it was the park ranger. His high beams flooded our backs, but we continued digging. We tried to act innocent, but we both knew what was coming.

"You boys know the park's closed?" he started.

I turned to face him.

"Yeah," I said sheepishly. "We were just going to go up and take a quick look."

He was undeterred. "Do you also know it's a federal offense to trespass in a national park?"

"Uh…" I started. That part I didn't know but had started to infer the answer.

John had finally found his jacket and joined the conversation in time to hear what the ranger said next. The guy seemed to be following some sort of questioning protocol.

He continued, "I need to ask you, do you have any firearms in your truck?"

John and I just looked at each other. I gulped.

You have to understand, John is a southern boy who had just completed multiple tours as an Army Ranger. Guns are tools of the trade and a way of life. He didn't just have one gun, he had many. And as for me, while I didn't know about the trespassing thing, I knew for sure it was illegal to have guns in a national park. We read each other's faces and silently agreed that honesty would be the best policy in this situation.

"Yes sir. I do." John replied. "I have a shotgun and an AR in the back, and a Sig P229 locked and loaded in the console."

The ranger's face went white as his hand reached for his side. I couldn't see if it was a radio or a gun of his own. "Uh, I'm going to need you to get all your weapons out and disassemble them on the hood," he replied. Things felt tense.

"Yes, sir," John said while I kicked rocks, trying to look as unsuspicious as possible.

John went to the cab to grab the Sig. The park ranger was nice enough, so I struck up a conversation in hopes of building rapport.

"We're just passing through on our way to Georgia," I said.

"You're a long way from Georgia," the ranger replied.

I could tell he was warming up, so I continued. John was grabbing the other weapons from the back.

"Yeah, my buddy here is headed home. He just got out of the army."

"Is that right?" he replied. I had piqued his interest.

At this point John placed the shotgun on the hood and gave me a glance. We could both tell where this was going.

"Yeah," John said. "Can't wait to get home."

"What did you do in the army?" The park ranger asked the question we both saw coming.

John replied, "Oh, I was a Ranger in the Second Battalion out of Fort Lewis…"

Before John even finished, I could see it. The effect was immediate and visible. The park ranger was starstruck. His disposition had officially changed.

"Ya don't say?" There was a giddiness in his voice.

This started a back and forth between the three of us. John shared some stories, and I slipped in how bummed we were to not be able to see the mountain. As the conversation wound down, the ranger told us to sit tight while he "called in the incident."

He ducked into his vehicle while John and I waited and wondered, his headlights shining on us the whole time.

"What is he calling in?" I asked.

"Not sure," John replied. "I guess we'll see."

We smirked at each other. This was exactly the kind of thing that made road trips an adventure, and we both knew it. After a few minutes, the ranger popped his head over the cruiser door.

"Okay, fellas," he started, "I'm gonna need you to keep those firearms disassembled until you exit the park." We breathed sighs of relief and expected to be on our way, but the ranger continued, "I just called Joe and he's gonna fire up the lights for ya, and I'll walk you up to see the monument."

"What!?" we said in unison. This was working out far better than we expected. We had trespassed on federal land in the middle of the night with loaded weapons, and they were going to illuminate Mount Rushmore *just for us*?

Minutes later, in pitch-black darkness, we crested the concrete knoll on our way up to see Mount Rushmore. As we did, the lights warmed up as if for dramatic effect. We reached the viewing area just in time to see Teddy, George, Tom, and Abe's shining faces light up. Just for us. Ah, road trips. Always an adventure indeed!

TOUGH TALKS AND UNEXPECTED ADVENTURE

I share this story because it's awesome, but also to illustrate how honesty in adversity can lead to unforeseen blessings, particularly when it would be easier to avoid a direct conversation, hide the truth, or water it down.

You and your wife are on a lifelong journey together, and just like setting out on a road trip, you're bound to have adventures. Some will be fun and others rough. Depending on how you process the difficult twists, they will either bring you together or drive you apart.

What might unexpected adventures look like in marriage? And do you have a predetermined mode of responding that governs what you will do? Consider the following unforeseen challenges couples face, then ask yourself, *How would I communicate through it?* (This is a communication book after all.)

- Sudden loss of your job
- Miscarriage or trouble conceiving children
- Death of one of your parents
- Confessing sin to your wife
- Your wife confessing sins against you
- Experiencing betrayal by a close friend
- Infidelity
- Life-altering sickness or injury

Many times when thinking through these kinds of scenarios, we wonder how we'd *respond*. Here, I'm asking you to consider how you'd *communicate* through it.

What honest conversations would you have?

How would you care for your wife?

How would you be attentive to her emotions? And yours?

Most importantly, how would you show your wife the character of Christ in how you speak to her and love her through it?

FREEDOM IS TRUTH

Choosing honesty isn't always about choosing not to lie. Most often, it's about choosing to face challenges head-on with eternity in mind and Christ in view. Then it's about speaking clearly and candidly as you process through it. Communicating honestly isn't always easy, but it's always right. And it can lead to unforeseen blessings (or adventures) for your marriage.

As John wrote, "God is light, and in him is no darkness at all" (1 John 1:5). Our God has not a drop of darkness in him, yet he chose to save sinners and draw them unto himself for their good and his glory.

The description of God being light is followed by an implication for those who profess him. John continued, "If we say we have fellowship with him while we walk in darkness, we lie and do not practice the truth" (1 John 1:6). Walking in darkness and professions of light cannot coexist. This means facing every manner of dark circumstance as light walkers, illuminated by the truth of Christ, confident in God's sovereignty, and at peace by the help of the Holy Spirit. There is freedom in the light because there's freedom in the truth. "You will know the truth, and the truth will set you free" (John 8:32).

On the flip side, if we consider ourselves light walkers (Christians), yet we walk void of truth, peace, or confidence in our loving Father, that makes us liars and "the truth is not in us." John's words, not mine.

SURE IN UNCERTAINTY

If you haven't yet faced difficulties like the ones I listed, you will. When you do, you have two decisions to make.

First, you must *choose* to walk in the light. Let the light of Christ's truth expose the dim and dark areas of your heart. Then, let the light of God's grace root out every drop of fear, shame, pain, sin, disappointment, doubt, or whatever other type of darkness you find. Not only will you be living honestly, but you'll be headed toward the results John described: fellowship with one another and cleansing from unrighteousness (1 John 1:7).

Second, both today and in that moment, decide that you will communicate *through* the darkness, whatever it is, and run back into the light. A couple centered on Christ and grounded in the gospel need only communicate and trust God as one in order to navigate from darkness to light. Stand boldly and speak honestly as a man whose confidence comes from being known fully and *still* loved by the God of light. Urge your bride to do the same. It is our blessed assurance in Christ that turns every catastrophe on its head and every disaster into a sanctifying, testimony-shaping adventure.

As a husband, I encourage you to be the first to behold the person and work of Christ in every challenge. Cling to Christ and let him be the filter through which you communicate with your wife.

John and I could have never anticipated the adventure we'd have that night at Mount Rushmore. There was no favor we could call in and no button to push to make it happen. Thankfully, providentially, and with honesty, the lights somehow turned on. And the view was better than we could have ever anticipated.

> **KEY TAKEAWAY**
> Communicating honestly isn't always easy, but it's always right.

MEDIOCRITY VS MASTERY

Mediocrity	*Mastery*
Content to walk in darkness when dealing with difficulty	Prepared to trust Jesus when stepping into the light and being honest
Avoids hard conversations in order to "keep the peace"	Sees communication as a vital means to process difficulty together
Minimizes the circumstance to avoid discomfort	Willing to face difficulty directly, hopefully, and with faith

APPLICATION QUESTIONS

Have you faced any of the difficulties listed in this chapter? How do you think you handled the surrounding conversations with your wife?

Based on your answer to the previous question, what are some tangible ways you might improve when facing future difficulty?

In your view, what are the greatest benefits to "walking in the light" with your wife through challenging circumstances? Describe a few.

CHAPTER FIFTEEN

THE MANNER AND THE METHOD
Why (and How) Love and Truth Must Coexist

> *Rather, speaking the truth in love, we are to grow up in every way into him who is the head, into Christ.*
> *Ephesians 4:15*

The Pauline notion of speaking truth in love was an ancient absurdity. It must've been, because it still seems that way today, at least in fleshly terms. In our culture, it feels impossible to speak truth *with* love because you're forced to choose between the two.

Some use love as a muzzle for anyone confronting sin (since doing so is offensive and, as the reasoning goes, unloving). Others brandish truth as a bludgeon, foregoing tact, nuance, and conversational breadth in the name of keeping to the facts. Indeed, conjoining truth and love is akin to tiptoeing a tattered tightrope over piranha-infested waters. Few succeed and those who do are rare and bloody.

Still, Paul's exhortation stands, so regardless of how difficult it seems, speaking truth in love *must* be possible. Not only is it possible, it's an imperative for those who aim to be faithful to Christ, especially husbands.

Here's the passage: "Rather, speaking the truth in love, we are to grow up in every way into him who is the head, into Christ" (Ephesians 4:15). I'd like to explore two components of this passage that I believe are instructive for how husbands communicate: the exhortation itself and the end he has in mind.

THE EXHORTATION

For Christians, the idea of speaking truth in love is commonplace. For the uninitiated, Paul is addressing the content of believers' speech to each other as well as the way they communicate. As one commentator notes, "The truth must not be used as a club to bludgeon people into acceptance and obedience must always be presented in love. The truth leads the Christian to maturity, which is defined here as growing up into Christ."10 This is in line with John's command in another letter, "Let us not love in word or talk but in deed and in truth" (1 John 3:18).

It is important to speak the truth, but it is also important to do so lovingly. Where either is absent, sin abounds. Seems simple, and it is, as long as we all agree on the verse's meaning and application. Thus, the rub. Assuming we agree on truth (the Bible) and love (as prescribed in the Bible), I'll get right to it.

For husbands, this verse means it's not adequate to simply say true things to our wives while disregarding how we say them. Why

---

10. Commentary on Ephesians 4:15 from The esv Study Bible (Wheaton, IL: Crossway, 2008), 2269.

is this so important? Because how you say something changes what's being communicated.

Consider the following illustration that shows how stressing different words changes the meaning of the sentence. The bolded words are where the stress should be placed.

I didn't buy my wife flowers. *(Then who did?)*
I **didn't** buy my wife flowers. *(I bought nothing.)*
I didn't **buy** my wife flowers. *(They're stolen.)*
I didn't buy **my** wife flowers. *(Whose wife then?)*
I didn't buy my **wife** flowers. *(Then who are they for?)*
I didn't buy my wife **flowers**. *(I got her something else.)*

It's simplistic, but it gets the point across. Even without my explainers, you would intuitively know the nuanced interpretation of each sentence. There are even nuances to the nuances depending on your personal lens, which is based on worldview, mood, biases, and blood sugar.

Now, given what we know about love from other passages, the methods by which we speak truth become even more clear. We are to speak in ways that are:

Patient,
Kind,
Not envious,
Not boastful,
Humble,
Not rude,
Not self-seeking,
Not irritable,
Not resentful,
…for starters (1 Corinthians 13:4–5).

If we are to speak lovingly, we must know how love would speak, and Love himself has spoken through his Son.

> Anyone who does not love does not know God, because God is love. In this the love of God was made manifest among us, that God sent his only Son into the world, so that we might live through him. In this is love, not that we have loved God but that he loved us and sent his Son to be the propitiation for our sins. Beloved, if God so loved us, we also ought to love one another. (1 John 4:8–11)

So to speak truth as love would speak, we look to the Word and we witness the life of Christ. That is the essence of Paul's exhortation to speak truth in love.

THE END IN MIND

Are we called to speak carefully and lovingly just so we might avoid conflict and drama? While that's a welcomed byproduct, it's not the goal. The endgame of speaking truth in love is so Christians—both individually and as a community—will mature and better resemble Christ. Paul wrote, "We are to grow up in every way into him who is the head, into Christ," so that "when each part is working properly, [God] makes the body grow so that it builds itself up in love" (Ephesians 4:15–16).

Speaking truth in love is not only a manner of communication, it's a method for sanctification. This is the foundation of Christian honesty. When I speak to you truly, I am speaking to you lovingly, because the more you mature in Christ, the more completely you slough off your old self, have your mind renewed, and adorn your new identity in him (Ephesians 4:20–24). Truthful love and loving truthfully are the seeds of sanctification sown among believers.

Of course, all the same can be said for your conversations with your wife.

AS BEFITS YOUR BELOVED

Any average husband can bluntly tell his wife the truth, but in order to "speak the truth in such a way that the spirit of love is maintained," there must be a real desire for the good of the other. This is how "love hopes all things" as Paul described (1 Corinthians 13:7). Does your manner of communication reflect the reality that you want the very best for your wife? Is your truth telling done in love with the endgame of your wife's sanctification in view? Let it be so, and you will be speaking truth to her in a manner that befits her *as your beloved*, so that she will be better for it, being molded by God's loving hand into the image of Christ.

> **KEY TAKEAWAY**
>
> Truth and love must coexist for marital communication to flourish. Wise husbands discern how to communicate truth in loving ways, no matter the topic.

MEDIOCRITY VS MASTERY

Mediocrity	*Mastery*
Speaks truth but is unloving in his manner of speaking	Speaks truth with high regard for both transmission and reception
Avoids hard truths in the name of keeping the peace	Willing to engage in difficult conversations to preserve truth
Blames wife for being too sensitive when she reacts negatively to truth spoken unlovingly	Takes responsibility for speaking unlovingly if applicable; seeks to grow

APPLICATION QUESTIONS

Do you struggle to speak truth with love? Why or why not? Do you tend to lean too heavily to either side?

How will you know when you have successfully spoken the truth with love? Be specific.

Speaking truth with love isn't a guarantee of a positive reaction. How will you respond if your wife responds adversely to hearing you speak the truth, even when you do so as lovingly as you're able?

CHAPTER SIXTEEN

THE CLIFF AND THE LOGJAM
Breaking Free from Communication Deadlock

*The heart of the godly thinks carefully before speaking;
the mouth of the wicked overflows with evil words.*
Proverbs 15:28 NLT

When cliff jumping into a river, you'll do well to avoid four major hazards. First, and most obviously, make sure the water is deep and free of obstructions. Second, research the river and avoid big rapids and waterfalls. Third, ensure the water isn't too cold, as your body can go into shock, which creates all sorts of problems. Fourth, avoid logjams because they'll kill you.

How do I know this? Mostly common sense, but also because cliff jumping was our favorite pastime growing up. My friends and I spent every free summer day possible piling into cars and scouring the wilderness for places to hurl our bodies through the air into water. Our hunt for adventure put us in peril more often than our moms knew, which was probably for the best.

One episode took the danger cake. While on a family camping trip, my friend Phil and I ventured down the Ohanapecosh River. It's a deep, tree-lined, icy, blue-green river fed by glacial runoff from Mount Rainier. I grew up swimming in its freshly thawed waters, but our typical spots had grown dull, so we took to exploring.

We hiked downstream until we spotted a choice cliff, and as an added bonus, there was a rock wall jutting out over the river, providing a novel way to reach the crag in question. I took to the wall, and it wasn't until I had passed the point of no return that I realized I had made a horrible mistake.

The wall was brittle, wet, and slick; my grip grew weaker with each new hold. I looked for an emergency bail-out route, but there were none. While I was only about twenty feet above the river, this improvised cliff jump spot fantastically failed my four-point safety inspection. Shallow water, raging rapids, glacial runoff, and as I discovered en route, a gigantic logjam downstream.

It's the logjam that terrified me the most. I'd survived shallow jumps, icy temps, and decent rapids before, but I knew this logjam would end me. I had heard stories of strong swimmers getting sucked beneath the surface and trapped in the branches below. Each of the fifty-plus logs made it clear that if I were to fall into the river and get washed into the jam, it would take an act of God to get to the other side alive. I suddenly understood why they're also called "deadlocks."

Thankfully, I didn't have to find out the hard way. It's remarkable how your grip strengthens when you might die. Somehow by the grace of God, I summoned the strength to complete the climb and scramble to safety. Now, every rock wall or logjam stands as a stark reminder of God's unmerited gift of a good grip.

MARITAL DEADLOCK

Logjams in marriage terrify me too. In times when Selena and I have had prolonged periods of disagreement, I've felt safe so long as the communication waters kept flowing unobstructed. It's whenever a communication deadlock occurs that I start to feel like I'm hanging on for my life again. The worst fight we've ever had was also the most silent. It went on for weeks, and I wondered if we'd ever be able to reconcile. Thankfully we did, but the risk of getting hung up and drowned under the surface had never felt so real. Left unmitigated, communication logjams will cut off intimacy, muck up every conversation, and kill the life and joy in your marriage.

The logs that make up marital logjams take familiar forms: apathy, cutting remarks, prolonged unforgiveness, mounting bitterness, past hurts, and scorekeeping are all personal, common examples. Together these logs form an impassable barrier to our unity and intimacy as a couple. But, as with literal logjams, the key to breaking the entire thing loose is plucking out the first log. Then, each subsequent log dislodges with greater and greater ease.

We'll talk about plucking out that first log in a moment, but first, let's consider how the jam happened in the first place.

HOW YOU GOT JAMMED

Consider the passage at the beginning of this chapter: "The heart of the godly thinks carefully before speaking" (Proverbs 15:28 nlt). Solomon is making an explicit connection between a man's godliness and his speech. And there's another connection between one's heart and his thinking. For many wives, thinking with the heart is intuitive. For many husbands, it's oxymoronic, like plastic silverware.

Clearly our wives are on to something. They've known it all along. Human intuition is real, discernment matters, and deep inexpressible truths do exist.[11] As husbands we'd be wise to let this proverb bear its full weight on our hearts, lest we let evil words gush from wicked maws.

Could it be that much of what jams communication in a marriage is the result of husbands detaching our holiness from how we speak, and dissociating our hearts from how we think? Think back to the last logjam you experienced in your marriage. What role did your careless words play in putting logs in place? And what role did your heartless thinking play in keeping them there?

LOG EXTRACTION

Thankfully, God gave us his living Word to inform our words and transform our minds. Logjams aren't inevitable, and as you mature in your marriage and communication you will face fewer of them. But, when you do find your conversational waterways obstructed, it's helpful to have tangible ideas for how to break jams apart to get things flowing again.

Here are three ideas I've discovered that bust jams good. My hope is that you'll find one or two you can reference in the future in the spirit of careful speech and heart-informed thinking.

---

11. If in doubt, try explaining the Trinity to a layperson.

1. Pray, recall, repent.

In the heat of a disagreement, it's easy to not see yourself objectively and fail to recognize where you've sinned against your wife. It could be pride, selfishness, or lack of introspection that causes you to not see your fault. Pray and ask the Holy Spirit to show you how you've not been careful with your words.

As he reveals things, repent to God, then repent to your wife and seek her forgiveness. This is most often the largest and most critical log to remove from the river, and this is what developing the godly heart-character looks like.

2. Confirm and clarify.

Spoiler alert, your wife isn't perfect. She'll contribute to the logjams just like you, but not always on purpose. Remember, if your wife says something upsetting, it's entirely possible that she meant something different than what you heard. This may be because of how she said it, or it might be based on how you received it. Try to pinpoint specific moments in your conversation where you felt a log being tossed into the river. If that moment was something your wife said, are you sure you heard her correctly?

A useful way to find out is to calmly ask, "I heard you say _____, and I thought you meant _____. Do I get it?" Many times just asking this question helps you see each other (and yourselves) more clearly, which inevitably gets your communication flowing again.

3. Set the stage to do the work.

Not all logjams are equally severe, but all require work to clear. Deadlocks never resolve themselves in a healthy way without conscious effort. And, if they do seem to be resolved without log removal, I'd argue that you've just forgotten what the issues were, and they'll be back when the next torrential downpour floods your riverbanks.

So set the stage to do the work. I recommend you start by praying for God to reveal any areas of your heart that need attention (this is different from the prayer objective above). What led to the behavior that brought about the jam in the first place? What are the underlying reasons for the logs themselves? Is there an infestation of fear, insecurity, frustration, shame, or doubt that could be causing your logs to rot? Pray for a soft heart and pray that God softens your wife's heart too. Then trust the Holy Spirit to convict both of you accordingly.

Next dig deep into Scripture. What passages speak to the heart issues at play? What stories and people of the Bible reveal the wisdom of God for your situation? There is no nook too deep or cranny too concealed for sin to hide from the light of God's Word. Shine it in there and let the roaches scatter.

Finally, discern how best to approach your bride and begin a new conversation. If she is willing, do your best to find a productive place to talk. No kids, no distractions, no interruptions. Make dinner, go out, or take a drive. Whatever works best for you, do it with a prayerful, hopeful heart that your log-plucking efforts will bear fruit.

RIPARIAN STEWARDSHIP

Communication is a constantly flowing river in every marriage. Debris will inevitably muck up the water as you weather life together. Don't sweat it, steward it. River maintenance is part and parcel of every marriage. If you're in a tough season currently or, whenever you face one in the future, you can initiate the work required to get the communication waters flowing again.

The work may include scheduling time with your wife to reconnect, have an honest talk, and pluck that first log. Or it may mean making an appointment with your pastor to get help with some of the heavy lifting. He may help you himself, or he may shepherd you alongside a biblical counselor. Whatever the work needed to clear the jam, simply start. Get that first log behind you and watch as communication begins to flow freely once again.

> **KEY TAKEAWAY**
> Left unmitigated, communication logjams will cut off intimacy, muck up every conversation, and kill the life and joy in your marriage.

MEDIOCRITY VS MASTERY

Mediocrity	*Mastery*
Allows "logs" to jam flows of communication and fails to recognize when it happens	Recognizes communication logjams and acknowledges their inherent danger
Assumes communication issues will resolve themselves, considers them resolved when really they've been forgotten or swept under the rug	Leads the unjamming process by taking steps to pluck out logs or get help as needed

APPLICATION QUESTIONS

Whether or not you've experienced a severe logjam in your communication, what sorts of logs are typical for your marriage?

Diseased logs grow in groves. For example, if your job is a consistent source of unhealthy stress and anxiety, it is likely contributing many logs to your marital jams. Are there any troublesome groves growing in your heart? Identify and describe them below.

CHAPTER SEVENTEEN

THE QUEST AND THE QUERY
Mastering the Art of Asking Good Questions

> *But the* LORD *God called to the man*
> *and said to him, "Where are you?"*
> *Genesis 3:9*

The ability to inquire sets humankind apart from the rest of creation. Even the world's most intelligent beasts—apes, dogs, pigs, and the like—are unable to ask basic questions, and it's not because they lack lingual dexterity.

Whereas children ask badly formed questions with their first grunts and utterances ("Can I have?" or "What that?") before their first birthday, scientists working with apes for years haven't been able to detect one question or even one sign of inquiry out of them. Why is that? What is it about the human mind that enables us to ask questions? While I won't be able to solve that particular mystery in this chapter, I do hope to awaken in your mind a fresh penchant for asking thoughtful questions in the interest of exceptional marital communication.

OUR QUESTIONING GOD

God hardwired into humanity our ability to ask questions, but why? Is it because we're made in his image? Perhaps. God himself does ask questions, but when he does, it's not for lack of knowing. This also rules out questions of curiosity. What could possibly make God, the omnipotent creator and sustainer of all, curious? Nothing comes to mind because everything's in his.

Why, then, does God inquire? Consider the first question God asks in the Bible, "But the Lord God called to the man and said to him, 'Where are you?'" (Genesis 3:9). This single inquiry gives us immense insight into the types of questions God asks and why.

The context of Genesis 3 is the fall. Adam and Eve had just eaten the fruit of the forbidden tree, and when they heard God walking through the garden, they hid. Whereas they used to walk the garden freely, with clear consciences and without clothes, they were now naked, ashamed, and terrified. They had done the one thing God had commanded them not to do. Their communion with God was shattered, and they felt the darkness creeping in.

Still, they were being pursued.

Lovingly, as God walked through the garden, he called out to Adam, asking, "Where are you?"

It's clear, God knew exactly where they were. He also knew *why* they were there. Information gathering wasn't God's objective. (How could it be?) God was reaching out to his beloved people with an invitation. He was inviting them toward repentance and reconciliation.

That's why God's first question is so profound. Instead of a cold pronouncement of the curse—which God would have been 100 percent justified in doing—we get a preemptive look at his graceful pursuit of mankind. God does ask questions of his creation, but his questions are of a rhetorical quality that points to his underlying reason: to unambiguously display his holiness, grace, and love.

This reveals much about God's character, but it also demonstrates what questions can do. Questions are uniquely powerful, and God has embedded in your very DNA the remarkable capacity to ask. Will you wisely wield the power to ask carefully crafted questions? I believe you can, because I'm sure you already have.

COPIOUS CURIOSITIES

Good questions are keys that open doors to new rooms of your relationship. Think back to your early encounters with your wife before you were married. How would you describe your first conversations? I'd bet my best laying hen that those first conversations were filled with curiosity, laughter, excitement, depth, discovery, and the twitterpated glow of young love in spring. Even if you were friends long before your romantic relationship began, those early weeks and months of your budding romance were markedly different. You were curious and you asked great questions.

Then, something happened. Your relationship progressed and at some point your curiosity waned. It wasn't on purpose, it just happened naturally as your knowledge grew and familiarity nestled in. And, don't get me wrong, familiarity is good and right for committed couples! In many ways, it's what makes the relationship feel like home. But when we lose curiosity, we stop asking questions. And if we stop asking questions long enough, we forget how to ask good questions.

Then, as the progression goes, when we forget how to ask great questions, we lose a vital communication skill along with the closeness it brings. Still, as with other skills in this book, asking good questions is a skill that can be learned and mastered. But first, let's explore what makes a question good.

THE QUEST FOR QUALITY QUESTIONS

Whoever said there's no such thing as a bad question needs to be questioned. Healthy couples learn to ask questions that match their relationship's maturity level.

When you were first dating, you were on a quest to gain information, so you asked things like, "Where did you grow up?" or "What hobbies do you enjoy?" or "What did you despise most about *The Kingdom of the Crystal Skull*?" If a husband is still asking those sorts of questions, something is amiss. Either his memory is bad, his situational awareness needs work, or both.

As your relationship matures, so should your questions. Sure, you'll still ask information-gathering questions, but the nature of the information you're gathering is very different. "How was your day?" is no longer just about what your wife did. It's about what she did, what she thinks, and how it's affecting her heart. And, depending on the conversation, it may even touch on the deepest level of interpersonal inquiry: beliefs.

Consider the layers of inquiry in the chart below.

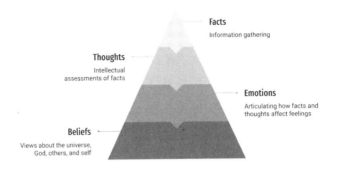

Quality questions that build marital intimacy inquire in such a way so as to get beneath facts and intellectual assessments into visceral emotional reactions and their underlying beliefs. Good questions take into account the full breadth of relational data available to husbands. They bring along with them your years-long history together while also acknowledging the current state of things.

What does your wife's intellectual view of her household responsibilities reveal about her feelings and beliefs? In what ways are her feelings about you informed by how she believes a husband should function? Do your thoughts about her relative's cancer diagnosis take into account your wife's emotions and beliefs about sickness and death? These are all questions which actively mine for meaning. And shared meaning means shared connection.

THE GOODNESS TO BE HAD

As we've established, your role in communication is analogous to your role as husband. Like every other communication habit and skill, thought and intentionality go far to bridge the chasm between mediocrity and mastery.

The first step toward better questions is understanding the role they play in deepening your relationship. Questions accomplish far more than gaining information. Becoming a good question asker can help your wife:

- Emotionally process difficult events in a healthy way
- Feel loved and cared for by you and by God
- Identify lies she believes that cause spiritual and emotional dissonance
- Diagnose doubt in God and distrust of his Word
- Remember the goodness and faithfulness of God despite life's circumstances
- Sort through relational conflict
- Experience emotional and intellectual breakthrough
- Discover how to apply God's Word in unclear situations

Of course, the above list is just a glimpse. Imagine the potential.

Asking insightful questions is an irreplaceable tool to plumb the depths of your wife's heart. This isn't even to mention the ancillary benefits you'll experience from the conversations had.

Alternatively, failing to ask quality questions can cause your bride to feel alone, unseen, frustrated, and unloved. Refuse to settle for mediocre questions. There is too much goodness to be gained.

Determine today to master the art of asking thoughtful questions with precision and care. Your wife will thank you, your communication quality will multiply, and you'll discover things about your bride you may have never known otherwise.

> **KEY TAKEAWAY**
> Good questions are keys that open doors to new rooms of your relationship.

MEDIOCRITY VS MASTERY

Mediocrity	Mastery
Allows familiarity to lead to complacency	Recognizes the need to continue pursuing one another in marriage
Is minimally curious about his wife	Sees wife as dynamic and growing, which drives curiosity
Asks mostly surface level questions to gather information	Asks questions as a means of gaining connection, insight, and growth

APPLICATION QUESTIONS

How can you lead your bride with greater, more selfless love through the ways you inquire? Remember that good questions do far more than reveal new information.

What is at stake if you don't regularly ask your wife thoughtful questions?

What practical steps can you take today to begin asking better questions?

CHAPTER EIGHTEEN

THE MOLD AND THE MAP
Intellect Is Mighty but Wisdom Is King

Look carefully then how you walk, not as unwise but as wise, making the best use of the time, because the days are evil. Therefore do not be foolish, but understand what the will of the Lord is.
Ephesians 5:15–17

Would you believe me if I told you that slime mold designed the Tokyo rail network? In 2010, a collective of Japanese scientists published a paper that seemed to indicate cellular intelligence in a species of slime mold called *Physarum polycephalum*, or "the blob" to those who know it.

This team of researchers set up an experiment where they placed an "individual plasmodium"—or one single-celled slime mold creature—on a substrate dotted with thirty-six food sources, which were laid out in a pattern similar to the Tokyo area. Each food spot represented a key geographic location served by the existing Tokyo rail system. Their findings were unreal.

Once dabbed upon the substrate, the little creature immediately got to work looking for food. For the first eight hours it spread out like an oil slick, getting thinner and thinner and radiating outward, blanketing over each food source as it passed. Throughout the next eight hours it reached the outer limits of the food source network and began to organize.

Over the next ten hours, *P. polycephalum* created a complex network of nutrient transportation tubes that interconnected each food source via the most efficient routes possible. Again, this is a *single-celled amoeboid goo*. Still, scientists observed it calculating the most efficient way to find and distribute vital nutrients from its surroundings. But that's not the mind-blowing part.

At the end of twenty-six hours, the scientists compared the mold map with the actual rail map of Tokyo and its surrounding cities. According to the study, the slime mold formed "networks with comparable efficiency, fault tolerance, and cost to those of … the Tokyo rail system."[12] Like I said, unreal.

The blob didn't just find the food and consume it. It created a map of interconnectedness that virtually matched the Tokyo railway map. To add insult to plasmodium-induced injury, *P. polycephalum* did it all in a day! I wonder how the Tokyo railway design team felt upon receiving the news?

It's spectacular, but what could this possibly have to do with communication in marriage? Glad you asked. It has to do with wisdom.

---

12. Atsushi Tero et al., "Rules for Biologically Inspired Adaptive Network Design," *Science* 327, no. 5964 (January 2010): 439, https://www.science.org/doi/10.1126/science.1177894.

WISE AS MOLD

There is a sense in which nature—even slime mold—exudes wisdom, because nature constantly glorifies God. Everything in the entire universe is fine existing *as it was created* except humankind. Elisabeth Elliot said it like this, "A clam glorifies God better than we do, because the clam is being everything it was created to be, whereas we are not."[13] As a rule, creation glorifies God. We are the exception.

At the triumphal entry, Christ's disciples cheered the glories of God, and when the Pharisees urged Jesus to quiet them, he told them that if he did, "the very stones would cry out" (Luke 19:37–40). Isaiah talked about mountains and hills breaking out in song and trees clapping their hands to the glory of God (Isaiah 55:12). The psalmist said, "The heavens declare the glory of God, and the sky above proclaims his handiwork" (Psalm 19:1). If wisdom is measured by glorifying God, creation is very wise, which is why I brought up the mold.

When I first read about *Physarum polycephalum* it made me think about the relationship between data and wisdom. The slime was placed on the substrate with no data. It knew nothing, so it spread out in search of information. It gained information by locating the food spots, then the mold adjusted to most efficiently consume the food and achieve its goals: survival and growth.

The blob is intelligent for slime, and in the sense described above, it's also *wise*. This is because mold doesn't have to choose to do what God designed it to do, it just does it. Contrarily, *choosing* to glorify God is not our factory setting. (To be clear, every atom and iota of creation *will* glorify God one way or

---

13. Timothy Keller with Kathy Keller, *The Songs of Jesus* (New York: Viking, 2015), 262.

another, it's just a matter of when. See Philippians 2:10–11.) In other words, we must choose to walk wisely lest we suppress the truth in unrighteousness, become futile in our thinking, and have darkened hearts (Romans 1:18–32).

This reality is ever evident in how you listen and speak to your wife. As you hear her voice, watch her body language, and factor in the surrounding circumstances—all of which are valuable nodes of information—you must not only choose the correct way to respond but you must choose *wisely* and in a way that glorifies God.

Your communication with your wife has much to do with your marital health, your loving headship, and the flourishing of your wife, but it's primarily about God's glory. In this way, it's about walking wisely. "Look carefully then how you walk, not as unwise but as wise" and "understand what the will of the Lord is" (Ephesians 5:15–17).

WISDOM IS AS WISDOM DOES

We just discussed wisdom as living in a way that glorifies God. The following aspects of wisdom should help you apply that definition to your husbandly communication.

Wisdom is an attribute of God.

Though you're not as wise *as* God, you can be wise *like* him since you bear his image. There's a difference in degree but similarity in kind. So, just as you can grow in holiness, you can grow in wisdom. Not only that, you are called to earnestly *seek* for wisdom as you would for silver and hidden treasures (Proverbs 2:4), so that you might "understand righteousness and justice and equity, every good path; for wisdom will come into your heart," so "discretion will watch over you" and "understanding will guard you" (Proverbs 2:9–11).

However confusing things seem, or however much you struggle to understand your wife, keep chasing wisdom. You have an built-in capacity for it, and you are called to pursue it as a treasure of utmost worth.

Wisdom fears God most.

Of the unrighteous, Paul writes, "For although they knew God, *they did not honor him as God* or give thanks to him, but they became futile in their thinking, and their foolish hearts were darkened. Claiming to be wise, they became fools" (Romans 1:21–22, emphasis added). Want to avoid a darkened heart? The only way is to fear God.

The first step to walking wisely is to fear him. "The fear of the Lord is the beginning of wisdom" (Proverbs 9:10). Some get caught up on the word "fear." It means simply that you know God is God and you are not. Honor God as God and revere him most. It's the required first stone on wisdom's path.

Wisdom obeys God.

In fearing God as God, obey. If you know the right, loving, God-honoring way to communicate but you still don't do it, that's folly. Wisdom requires obedience to reap wisdom's reward. Doing and thinking otherwise will reap a fool's reward.

Wisdom has eternal perspective.

You and your wife will live forever, and you will answer to God for how you handle her heart. Wisdom would remind you of those truths as you carry out your day-to-day, temporal communication within your covenant. See Colossians 3:19, 1 Timothy 5:8, 1 Peter 3:7, and Ephesians 5:22 to learn more.

Wisdom is a sign of maturity.

Job said, "Wisdom is with the aged, and understanding in length of days" (Job 12:12). Don't be discouraged when you bungle communication with your wife. Dust yourself off, get up, and take another step with wisdom. Some wisdom comes through trial and error, while some comes with age and time. Keep pursuing it as the treasure it is.

SMARTER THAN SLIME, BUT WISER?

Our world is an information fire hose and we're all just trying not to drown in the deluge. The last thing we need is more information. Instead, we need wisdom. Which begs me to ask: You're smarter than slime mold, but are you wiser? I believe you are.

What makes one a wise communicator in marriage is simply this: fearing God and loving your wife. It really is that simple. After those two things, the particulars tend to fall into place. "The beginning of wisdom is this: Get wisdom. Though it cost *all you have*, get understanding" (Proverbs 4:7 NIV, emphasis added).

> **KEY TAKEAWAY**
>
> What makes one a wise communicator in marriage is simply this: fearing God and loving your wife.

MEDIOCRITY VS MASTERY

Mediocrity	*Mastery*
High regard for self; seeks knowledge as power	Fears God; seeks wisdom as a means to love
Responds with worldly wisdom	Responds with godly wisdom, considering words, tone, timing, and circumstance in light of the gospel

APPLICATION QUESTIONS

Given the chapter you just read, how would you describe wisdom in your own words? What does it mean to be a wise man?

If fearing God is the beginning of wisdom, what does it mean to fear God?

How does being a wise man change how you hear what your wife says? How does it change your response?

FINAL WORDS

I said it at the beginning, but it's worth repeating: improving your communication is your most potent and immediate opportunity to improve your marriage. Every aspect of your relationship hinges on it, including maintaining a deep connection, dealing with the various issues of marriage, and overcoming whatever difficulties you'll face. It's my prayer that the tools and ideas covered in this book will serve you well now and for the rest of your life. But, there's a catch.

Improved communication in itself has the ability to move the needle, but any progress you make must be undergirded by the truth of the gospel and a living faith in Jesus Christ. Otherwise, you'll never overcome the gravitational pull toward dysfunction. What do I mean? The gospel addresses the heart, and at the very core, every aspect of communication comes down to the heart.

Consider the words of Christ, "But what comes out of the mouth proceeds from the heart, and this defiles a person. For out of the heart come evil thoughts, murder, adultery, sexual immorality, theft, false witness, slander. These are what defile a person" (Matthew 15:18–20). It's not just about the words that proceed through the mouth, it's about how words come from the same heart that brings forth slander, lies, evil thoughts, sexual immorality, and even murder. It's possible to fake heart change by modifying how you speak, but is it real? No. Is it sustainable? I don't think so, at least not in a meaningful way. So, for communication to change for good, the heart must be changed for good. For communication to be renewed for good, the heart must be renewed for good. This begs the question, How does one change their own heart?

You can't, but God can.

This is precisely what Ezekiel prophesied when he quoted God saying, "I will give you a new heart and put a new spirit in you; I will remove from you your heart of stone and give you a heart of flesh" (Ezekiel 36:26 NIV). God is in the business of carving out cold, dead hearts and replacing them with living, soft ones. The old covenant had proven insufficient to save, so God promised to step in and do the saving himself, through a new covenant in Christ.

This is echoed and amplified by Jeremiah,

> Behold, the days are coming, declares the LORD, when *I will make a new covenant* with the house of Israel and the house of Judah, *not like the covenant that I made with their fathers* on the day when I took them by the hand to bring them out of the land of Egypt, *my covenant that they broke, though I was their husband*, declares the LORD. For this is the covenant that I will make with the house of Israel after those days, declares the LORD: I will put my law within them, and *I will write it on their hearts*. And I will be their God, and they

shall be my people. And no longer shall each one teach his neighbor and each his brother, saying, 'Know the LORD,' *for they shall all know me*, from the least of them to the greatest, declares the LORD. For I will forgive their iniquity, and *I will remember their sin no more*. (Jeremiah 31:31–34, emphasis added)

Praise be to our merciful God, the author of creation and the originator of the gospel! He has seen fit to give new hearts to unfaithful people. He has taken our hearts of stone and sewn into our chests new hearts of flesh. How?

Enter Jesus Christ.

The same Christ who said that the evil which proceeds from the heart is the same evil that defiles also graciously gives a new heart to anyone who places their trust in him. All they need to do is ask him, because he was not merely a wise teacher—Jesus Christ is God in the flesh (John 1:14), and he came so that all who believe in him might be saved (John 3:16–17). This is an incredible reality we must never forget.

Only Christ has the power to change your heart, and the good news is that he is also willing. We need only to ask. As Christ said, "Ask, and it will be given to you; seek, and you will find; knock, and it will be opened to you. For everyone who asks receives, and the one who seeks finds, and to the one who knocks it will be opened" (Matthew 7:7–8).

So, fellow husband, I commend you for this work with this one, massive caveat. Do your very best in your communication efforts, but never make the mistake of laboring absent the touch of Christ. Do the work, but do so from a heart made of flesh and given through Christ.

Trust him. Ask him. And labor alongside him as you love your bride just as he has loved his, the church (Ephesians 5:25). Then, I pray that by the words you say to your wife, you will prove to her, breath by breath, again and again, how profoundly loved she is in Christ.

ALSO AVAILABLE

Husband in Pursuit and *Wife in Pursuit* offer a gospel-centered path for couples who want to learn to creatively love each other as Christ has loved them. Over thirty-one days, you and your wife will dive into God's Word, rediscover how Christ has pursued you, and take intentional action to pursue each other.

Take the 31-Day Pursuit Challenge together.

Learn more at 31DayPursuit.com

ALSO AVAILABLE

Prayer is your first and most powerful weapon when fighting for your marriage. What could happen if you diligently and consistently sought God's heart for your wife? How different would your marriage be?

This bundle is written to help couples learn the habit of praying for one another through the many seasons of marriage.

Learn more at 40Prayers.com

ADDITIONAL RESOURCES

ABOUT US

Fierce Marriage exists to point couples to Christ and commission marriages for the gospel. That one mission drives everything we do, this book included. In addition, we produce content daily via our podcast, blog, and on social media.

THE FIERCE MARRIAGE PODCAST

Listen in every week as Ryan and Selena discuss modern marriage issues in light of the gospel. Subscribe and listen on iTunes, Spotify, or anywhere else podcasts are found.

FIND US ONLINE

Website: FierceMarriage.com
Email: FierceMarriage.com/List
Facebook: /FierceMarriage
Instagram: @FierceMarriage
YouTube: /FierceMarriage
Twitter: @FierceMarriage

ON-DEMAND MARRIAGE COURSES

We have a suite of marriage courses available for couples and churches. Please visit GospelCenteredMarriage.com to learn more.

DO YOU HAVE FEEDBACK OR A STORY?

If this book has helped you, please share your story with us. If we can improve or fix anything about this resource, please let us know by sending an email to care@fiercemarriage.com.

WANT TO LEAVE A REVIEW?

If you've enjoyed this book, we'd be honored if you wrote an honest review wherever you purchased your copy (on our website, Amazon.com, or elsewhere). Make sure to share how God is working in your marriage. You never know who might read it and be encouraged.

GROUP STUDY LEADERS

If you would like to lead a small group based on this book, bulk discounts are available (8+ copies). Please email details to care@fiercemarriage.com and someone will be in touch.

SPEAKING REQUESTS

Ryan and Selena are happy to work alongside churches and event organizers to bring gospel-centered hope and help to couples around the world through relatable teaching.

For speaking inquiries, visit FierceMarriage.com/Speaking.

FIERCE PARENTING

Find Christ-centered parenting resources at FierceParenting.com, including a podcast, e-books, articles, and more.

Do not merely listen to the word,
and so deceive yourselves.
Do what it says.

James 1:22 NIV